7 Secrets Every Woman Should Know

Copyright © 2009 Asia M. Hadley

All rights reserved. Printed in the U.S.A. No part of this publication may be reproduced or transmitted in any form or by any means, electronic or mechanical, including photocopy, recording or any information storage and retrieval system now known or to be invented, without permission in writing from the publisher, except by a reviewer who wishes to quote brief passages in connection with a review written for inclusion in a magazine, newspaper or broadcast.

Published in the United States by
Beckham Publications Group, Inc.
P.O. Box 4066, Silver Spring, MD 20914

ISBN: 978-0-9823876-9-6

0-9823876-9-5

Library of Congress Control Number: 2009934464

7 Secrets Every Woman Should Know

How to Create a Joy-Filled Life

Asia M. Hadley

PUBLICATIONS GROUP, INC.
Silver Spring

Acknowledgments

I am blessed that the Divine Creator gave us universal principles and laws to work with in order to co-create our reality.

I would like to thank my husband, Patrick Hadley, who shared his computer, provided emotional and physical space for me to work, and who always sees the best in me.

To my parents James and Curtixine Muhammad for always supporting and encouraging me to keep my spiritual life first and to be happy.

To my sister Dr. JaDawn Muhammad who continues to be an example of class and strength. Thank you for always speaking the truth and for keeping my best interest at heart. I especially want to thank your friends for being supportive of us both over the years. Special appreciation goes to: Dr. Monica Kelsey Brown, Donneva Falson, Cousin Ceth Jewell, Rhonda Kelsey, LiShunda Patterson, LaTonya (King) Thompson, Dr. Khyana Pumphrey, and Dr. Charisse Sekyi.

To my grandmother "Madea," Luvennia Robertson, a wise matriarch who teaches by example and makes all of her grandchildren feel like they're her favorite.

I send love to my Aunts Yvonne Ali, Celestine Beauchamp, Kathy Crayton, Helen Guy, Juanita Hasan, Annette Langford, Ayesha

Mahmoud, Lilly Mae Wingo, Vickie Wilburn, Sheila Williams and all of my great aunts.

Much love also goes to my Uncles Rachman Ali, Alfred Beauchamp, Dwight Crayton, Aspen "Pumpkin" Guy, Charles Ward, and Derrick Williams on whose shoulders I stand, including those who have transitioned, Moneta (Grandmother) and James (Grandfather) Crayton, Enwood Robertson (Grandfather), Aunts Doris "Fuzz" Gill, Virline Harris, Luvennia "Doll" Salaam, Brenda Ward, Uncle Benson Robertson and all of my other ancestors.

A big hug goes to my many cousins particularly, Tara Ali, LaCesha Edwards, Jamal Jewell, Stephanie Langford, Marriandra Robertson, Kesha Williams, and Anitra Zafari, who made growing up just plain fun!

Cousins Portia, Joe, Chase, and Cole Migas, thank you for being such great hosts throughout the years.

It's great to have reconnected with my cousins Denise and Sultan Muhammad and Tina, Wilbur, Jessica, Jordan, and Joshua Hewing.

Elaine, my hardworking sister-in-law, I know that Mr. and Mrs. Hadley are smiling from above.

Thank you to my Community family, Shafiqua Ameen, Lady Campbell, Sarah Grant-Rowe, Zakiya and Tony Courtney, Sharon Davis, Brother Kwabena Falson, Debra and John Fields, Mrs. Margaret Green, Reuben Harpole, Linda Jackson, Heddie Keith, Pamela Brown Mathis, Harriet McKinney, Brother Oshi, Francis Pitts, Former Mayor Marvin Pratt, Cheryl Shelby, Taki Raton, LaTrice Everett Robinson, ReDonna Rogers, Hattie Daniels-Rush, Bob Rush, Sister Minimah Shaheed, Dorthy Travis, Annette Polly Williams, Edith Adekunle Wilson, Cousin Maxine Wooten Lawrence, and community ancestor, Kathy Harrell Patterson.

Acknowledgments

My Spiritual Mother, Dr. Barbara Lewis King, Founder and Spiritual Leader of Hillside International Truth Center, my home away from home: I love you, I bless you, I appreciate you, and I thank God for you!

Marion Delaney-Harris and Hillside's Spirit of Sisterhood members, thank you for your friendship and sister chats, and for trusting me as chair. Special thanks to support group members, Cleopatra Bell, Elsa Celestine, Barbara Faison, Cecilia Harris, Paulette Jones, Kym Kennedy, Deborah Mills, Juanita Moore, Dorothy Scott, Melba Smith, Yolanda Neals, Juanita Wesley, and Nina Winston.

Melanie Magruder, your walk is a testament of the possibilities for those with faith and who are willing to take action. Thank you for taking up the gauntlet. You along with our core Toastmasters members, Corliss and Rashad Cook, Danita McClain, Mary Richardson, and Clem Washington made honing my speaking skills a blast!

Anita Plotinsky, Pattie Johnson, Shana Lightfoot, Fabiola Charles, and Harriet Khur, I value the doors that you all have opened for me to connect in Atlanta's nonprofit community.

I extend gratitude to Kayron Bearden, Joanne Kepics, Debbie Kirk, Melanie Callenbach, and Stephen Sherman for contributing to a harmonious work environment, which left me with sufficient energy to write after hours.

To Shalonda Trice, my early writing partner who agreed to "just be there" with me to write without asking me questions about what I was writing, because at the time, I didn't know, I was simply writing.

Anika Francis, my spiritual sister and warrior queen, thank you for your consistent demonstration of self-love and discipline through the writing and re-writing of this book.

Kyle Malone, I'm still learning from the example you set as a supervisor. And Tasha, I still crack up when I think of how we hid out in the car to escape "that seminar." I pray that mine are better.

I acknowledge my Indianapolis University-Purdue University at Indianapolis (IUPUI) support team for being a source of encouragement: Dr. Dwight Burlingame, Nina Gondola, Afia Griffith, Tanya Johnson, Marsha Currin McGriff, Aisha Miller, Kemi Ogidan, Alicia Roberts, Larry Smith, and Danielle Tyler.

To Sanura Ali and Linda Clemons, two dynamic women who helped light the way.

Love to Jahannah Sistrunk, my anchor who pushed and cheered me through the second writing of this book.

Much appreciation goes to the Gascoigne family, particularly Roxene for sharing her space and wonderful friends during my student exchange in Jamaica.

Ysanne Latchman, is one of the most "thought-full" friends that I have and whose delicious writing is always a source of inspiration.

Sherria Ards, LaToya Cole, and Nikeia McFarlane, three sister friends who patiently listened as I talked and talked about this book, and who believed me and in me!

To Drs. Dana and Sharon Dennard for creating a community space that nourished my mind, body, and spirit.

I'm grateful to my mentor, Brother Yirser Ra Hotep, for opening the door of wisdom to the teachings of Kemetic Yoga.

Tiffany Prewitt-James, thank you for joining me on the last leg of my writing journey. Coming to your house to write before I left for work intensified the joy in my day.

Aisha Iman, Damaris Hardiman, and Sharaye Smith, your creative energies are contagious!

I send love to Billy, Johnsie, James, and Jacob Cogman. It was in your basement that I first began writing this book.

Acknowledgments

I appreciate Sister Madeline Hatim, Bilal, Muhammad, Islah, Lamont, and Safia for being my loving God family from my early college years to the present.

Barry Beckham, my publisher, your patience is now legendary and your encouragement and expertise is unmatched. Thank you to Nanette Littlestone for your editorial assistance and for providing thought provoking feedback that stretched me.

I extend heartfelt gratitude to my mentors from afar: Queen Afua, Dr. Na'im Akbar, Dr. Maya Angelou, Tyra Banks, Dr. Michael Beckwith, Sarah Ban Breathnach, Les Brown, Deepak Chopra, Dr. Steven Covey, Edwine Gaines, Debrena Jackson Gandy, Louise Hay, Jerry and Esther Hicks, Rev. Deborah Johnson, Dr. Dennis Kimbro, Natasha Munson, Lisa Nichols, Dr. Alexander Pattakos, Anthony Robbins, Jewell Diamond Taylor, James Arthur Ray, Dr. Zhi Gang Sha, Iyanla Vanzant, Marianne Williamson, Oprah Winfrey, and Gary Zuchav.

To President Barak Obama and First Lady Michelle Obama for blazing a trail that will be remembered for generations to come. I'm so proud to live in this day and time to witness this historic presidency.

I am grateful for the support of countless number of relatives and friends who helped my dream to come true; though too numerous to name, I love you all the same.

Lastly, I'd like to thank the educational institutions that played a major role in shaping who I am today: Sister Clara Muhammad School, E.L. Phillips Elementary, Hartford Avenue, Roosevelt Middle School of the Arts, Whitefish Bay High School, St. Andrew High School for Girls, Florida A & M University, Light Streams for Better Living, and IUPUI.

Please forgive any errors or omissions in this book.

Contents

Acknowledgments 5
Introduction 13

Secret #1: Regular Expression of Gratitude Inspires Joy... 15

Secret #2: Your Inner World Shapes Your Outer World 34

Secret #3: Your Mood is a Habit 53

Secret #4: You are the Center of Your Universe 70

Secret #5: Become Your First Best Friend........................... 83

Secret #6: Meditate to Elevate 99

Secret #7: Co-creation Takes Place Consciously or
by Default 113

Conclusion 129

Introduction

7 Secrets Every Woman Should Know: How to Create a Joy-Filled Life is designed for the nourishment of mind, body, and spirit, and to support you in acting in accordance with your Divine life plan.

One of the main purposes of your life's journey is to listen to that inner voice of wisdom and find the courage and strength to follow its guidance. This journey requires self-knowledge, faith, and commitment to traverse through life's terrain. When you listen to that sacred voice within, you discover the joy that has always been there. You can access it at anytime. Regardless of your situations and circumstances, it's always available to you. Without this understanding, you put your overall well-being in the hands of others and leave it to chance conditions. *7 Secrets Every Woman Should Know* will help you rediscover your inner voice without sacrificing the joy you deserve.

You can liberate your mind by understanding the inner power to transform yourself and your life. Accept that you are a Divine manifestation of God who is within all of us. We are simple drops of water, while God is the ocean. We are made from the same substance but in an individualized smaller form. We have the potential to tap into the vast divine mind that operates through spiritual principles or universal laws.

If you are reading this book, it means that your mind is already open and receptive to the sharing of different perspectives. In the following chapters you'll discover tools and techniques to practice gratitude; create the environment you want; choose your mood; align your thoughts, feelings, and actions; honor and respect yourself; and consciously co-create a new paradigm of awareness, intent, and self-actualization. It is my sincere intent that these words inspire and uplift you as you walk through life with the support of family, friends, ancestors and a host of invisible beings that only have your good at heart.

May you continue to recognize the blessings in your life and allow them to flow!

Secret #1:
Regular Expression of Gratitude Inspires Joy

Gratitude unlocks the fullness of life. It turns what we have into enough, and more. It turns denial into acceptance, chaos to order, confusion to clarity. It can turn a meal into a feast, a house into a home, a stranger into a friend. Gratitude makes sense of our past, brings peace for today, and creates vision for tomorrow.
—**Melody Beattie**

Gratitude comes from the Latin word *gratis*, meaning thankful. If you add the letter "t" after the first "a" in gratitude and drop the "gr," the new word created is attitude. Gratitude is a state of mind in which your attitude is one of thankfulness and appreciation. To have an attitude of gratitude means to have a habit of seeing the good in circumstances and in people. Gratitude focuses the mind on the blessings present in your life. If you stopped to appreciate your material and nonmaterial abundance as well as the beauty in nature, you will resonate with vibrations that harmonize with feelings of joy.

One of the great laws of the universe is the law of vibration, which states that everything material and nonmaterial has a frequency, including your thoughts. Based on the law of attraction, which is a manifestation of the law of vibration, energies that are alike attract each other. Therefore, you connect with similar vibrations that feed the continuation of your joyous feelings when you are being appreciative. Do you see how complaining or talking negatively about yourself or others attracts similar energy to you? You are complaining when you knowingly talk to someone who can't help you resolve an issue. When you speak disparagingly about yourself or someone else, you find more to complain about because you are resonating with that energy level. Ultimately you attract situations and circumstances that reflect your consciousness.

In *Power vs. Force,* Dr. David Hawkins calibrates human levels of consciousness. He describes the lowest level as shame and progresses upward 16 levels to enlightenment. An individual can operate on various levels in different areas of life. Dr. Hawkins cites levels below 200 as destructive of life in both the individual and society while levels above 200 are positive manifestations of power. Energies such as peace, joy, and courage calibrate above 200 while fear, apathy and shame calibrate below 200. Whether you choose to believe the calibrated figures or not, you know you feel better when you have positive emotions rather than negative ones. Although not a prerequisite, feeling good often precipitates behaving kindly to yourself and others. Cultivating a spirit of gratitude is a way to keep your positive energy flowing.

Having a spirit of gratitude means you acknowledge and express appreciation for everything in your life such as your present circumstances, health, body, friends and foes. We all teach each other lessons. People and circumstances are mirrors that reflect what is happening in your inner world. This is your sanctuary of private thought where the subconscious exerts a great deal of control.

We have a tendency to express gratitude when we receive something tangible, when someone does something for us, ceremoniously before eating, and when things are going our way. Expressing gratitude for material things and positive circumstances is one way to express gratitude. A friend sent this delightful e-mail about being thankful:

I am thankful:
For the wife
Who says it's hot dogs tonight,
Because she is home with me,
And not out with someone else.

For the husband
Who is on the sofa
Being a couch potato,
Because he is home with me
And not out at the bars.

For the teenager
Who is complaining about doing dishes
Because it means she is at home,
Not on the streets.

For the taxes I pay
Because it means
I am employed.

For the clothes that fit a little to snug
Because it means
I have enough to eat.

Another more enduring approach to feeling gratitude is to focus on simply being grateful. Your expression of gratitude, therefore, is not tied to any specific circumstance or outcome. Being grateful for nature, life itself, and each new day are examples unrelated to circumstances.

Developing the habit of gratitude requires awareness. Frustration or some other unpleasant feeling can occur deceptively fast, so stay alert to negative shifts in your mood. You must also recognize the source of your negative feelings, which comes from the meaning you give to situations. As the saying goes, it's not what happens to you, it's how you think about what happens that influences your response the most.

I'll be the first to admit how challenging it can be to see beyond the appearance of a situation in order to find lessons and blessings, especially when you are in the midst of the storm.

Shortly after my husband Patrick and I relocated to Atlanta we began searching for homes to buy. I soon found the perfect area in a newly developing subdivision. The only thing we needed was a job for my husband. Every weekend we drove through the area observing the progress of the community. We toured the model homes. I visualized our children running down the stairs in the house and my walking with my slippers on the hardwood floors in the kitchen. The intricately speckled patterns in the granite countertops in the kitchen called out to me. With each site visit, my desire to move out of our apartment into a newly built home grew. A storm was brewing in my mind. As home lots sold, the more anxious to move I became. After all the lots were sold and homes were built in that community, I temporarily suspended our search.

A few months later while I was in Milwaukee visiting my family, Patrick, who was still searching for homes, discovered a new subdivision. I was open to resuming our search, so he took me to visit. We walked through several of the new homes, and I found one that was perfect for us. Once again, I visualized our children running down the stairs in the house and my walking with my slippers on the hardwood floors in the kitchen. The granite countertops in the kitchen called out to me again. I fell in love with this house. By this time, however, I had quit my job at a top staffing agency, so my husband and I were both looking for jobs. Luckily, within a few weeks I found a great position and we were able to move forward with the purchase of our home. Although it took several more months for my husband to find a job, when he did, it was a perfect fit for him because of what was about to happen in our lives.

A few weeks after accepting a faculty position at a university, Patrick's father's prostate cancer returned with a vengeance. Within a month, his father was in hospice care. As a professor, my husband does not have to teach everyday; therefore, he has at least two days off per week. During his first semester he had Wednesdays and Fridays off. The flexibility in his schedule allowed him to fly to Columbus, Ohio after his class on Thursday evenings and to return late Monday afternoon, in time for his class. Had Patrick landed any of the other jobs for which he applied, he would not have had this flexibility.

By the time we moved into our new home, housing prices dove sharply. Had we purchased when I originally desired, we would have paid a significantly higher price. Besides, the location of our current home is closer to both of our jobs, which means less time on the road. God's time is Divine time! It takes patience to wait on God. As you wait, various feelings may emerge. By writing what you are feeling and thinking down in a journal, you can obtain clarity about what thoughts you need to think in order to stay in alignment with your desire.

One of the quickest and easiest ways to cultivate inner joy is to keep a gratitude journal. By maintaining a gratitude journal, you have a selection of material from which to read during the times when you need it most. Because we can think only one thought at a time, gratitude focuses the mind on positive thoughts. If you are in the midst of inwardly or outwardly expressing appreciation, you cannot simultaneously long for what you don't have. Yearning breeds a sense of lack and a sense of lack feeds feelings of deficiency. In essence, you are saying to the universe, "I don't have enough!"

Several years ago, my mother, sister, and I sat in the den of my parent's home and conducted our SAVY Sister Circle meeting. SAVY is an acronym for Study Abroad Voyages for Youth. We founded SAVY to raise money to support youth who travel to the African Diaspora. Although the organization has been on hiatus for several years and I moved from Milwaukee, we still call our once- a-week prayer meeting our SAVY Sister Circle to ensure that we talk weekly.

During this meeting, I was feeling despondent and frustrated because I felt confused about what I wanted to do with my life. I was in my mid-twenties, jobless, and unsure of my direction. I melted like a five-year-old whose candy was taken away. With my hands cupped over my eyes, I sobbed uncontrollably. I was nearly $1,000 behind in paying my car note and behind in many of my other bills. I had been struggling for months to keep my head above water so that I could avoid drowning in my swelling sea of debt. Though I wasn't paying rent, my bills were still overwhelming. I was doing what I enjoyed. I was traveling to various schools to teach yoga and etiquette skills to middle school students, but income was sporadic. I was trying to be an entrepreneur but I could barely stomach the lack of income during slower periods. I shouted, "I can't do this, I need money!"

My entrepreneurial fantasy had turned into a living nightmare. What I really needed was the steady income of a job, at least for a while. Knowing that you have a consistent paycheck every two weeks can be a source of pseudo security for your psyche.

My ego had been so battered that I could barely think a positive thought. A lot of prayer for direction in my life and watching the *Oprah* show helped to lift me out of what Zig Ziglar calls stinkin' thinkin'. It was Oprah who reminded me about the gratitude journal. After spending quiet time in prayer, I wrote:

> *I must be grateful for all of my blessings, skills and talents. I am thankful for working out today at Le Club. I am thankful for earning a scholarship to attend Indiana University, Purdue University Indianapolis (IUPUI) to earn a dual master's degree in philanthropic studies and non-profit management. I am thankful for being able to type on this computer in front of me. I am thankful that the man I want to spend the rest of my life with just called me and would love for me to call him after I have finished writing. I am grateful for my health. I am thankful for writing today. I am thankful that I still have the sense to be grateful although I'm really pissed off!*

Regular Expression of Gratitude Inspires Joy

Expressing gratitude, particularly when you have negative emotions, helps you to get in touch with your feelings. Though you may be experiencing discomfort you can still honor your feelings while recognizing the blessings still present.

Over the years, I had been in and out of the habit of keeping a journal. Sometimes I expressed gratitude, more often I expressed daily irritations. For example, I wrote about my lack of steady income, choking in tennis, and deals I did not close. And the list goes on. My maudlin journal entries had directed my attention to all that was wrong with my life. I didn't understand that by writing every negative detail, I was attracting more to be negative about.

Through trial and error and monitoring my moods, I learned to express in writing what was bothering me, but quickly moved on by focusing on solutions or the lessons learned. Before I began focusing my writing on gratitude, my past writing reflected a perception of my life that left me stuck. I was unable to move forward and didn't clearly understand that I had to take full responsibility for my life experiences.

I reinstituted the practice of journal writing on the evening of my meltdown. When I started my gratitude journal, I immediately recognized a change in my attitude. I became more loving and patient with myself because I saw all that I had, from my health to making it to the post office right before it closed. When I began to list all of the things I was grateful for each day, I realized exactly how blessed I was. I redirected my attention to the positive aspects of my world.

Professors Robert A. Emmons and Michael E. McCullough, researchers at the University of California, Davis and the University of Miami, respectively, did long-term research on the nature of gratitude, its causes and its potential consequences for human health and well-being. Their research suggests that people who kept gratitude journals on a weekly basis:

- Exercised more regularly
- Reported few physical symptoms
- Felt better about their lives as a whole

- Had more optimism about the upcoming week compared to those who recorded hassles or neutral life events
- Reported making progress toward important personal goals over a two-month period
- Were more likely to report having helped someone with a personal problem or having offered emotional support to another

Keeping a gratitude journal helps me to keep perspective. Like many of you, I tend to magnify the negative and minimize the positive. This is particularly the case if I experience something negative near the time I am asked how my week is going. By tracking my positive feelings and happenings in my life, I have proof that things are better than my mind would have me to believe.

In *The Paradox of Choice: Why More is Less*, Barry Schwartz cites psychological phenomena like *prospect theory and counterfactuals* to help readers understand how common thinking processes alter our perceptions and feelings. Prospect theory explains how people evaluate circumstances and experiences relative to a standard, whether real or imaginary. So, in order to determine or understand how you or others process an experience, find out what comparison they are using. According to Schwartz, people evaluate their experiences compared to one or more of the following:

- What they hoped it would be
- What they expected it to be
- To other experiences they have had in the recent past
- Experiences that others have had

I'm sure you have made these comparisons based on a certain standard, whether you were conscious that you were making them or not.

Schwartz also discusses counterfactual thinking, which creates a "contrast between a person's actual experience and an imagined alternative." People can counterfactual upward or downward. Visualizing how much better an experience could have been is an example of upward counterfactual thinking. When you imagine a worse case scenario you are employing downward counterfactual thinking. If I find myself complaining about the quality of my car, for example, I think about how it is paid off and how I have a choice whether to take public transportation or not. When I counterfactual downward, by thinking about individuals who don't have a choice to drive, I immediately become grateful. You can use these concepts to help you remember the blessings present in your life. No matter the situation, there is always a silver lining, even when you're too distraught to look for it.

    I found relief when I learned about prospect theory and counterfactual thinking. I used them naturally although I didn't have terms to describe these ways of thinking. Using prospect theory and counterfactual thinking has helped me become more aware of my comparisons and thought patterns. When I start to compare my purchasing power to how much more others can buy, I quickly redirect my attention to being grateful for what I have and think about how others are dealing with a lot more serious issues than not being able to obtain the latest handbag. I can now strategically use these concepts to help moderate how I think and feel.

    I notice that I feel more empowered when I'm moving toward my desires instead of away from an undesirable situation. Some people are motivated to move toward what they want, while others are motivated to move away from what they don't want. In the same way, our wanting or yearning is more empowering when it comes from wanting something versus not having it. Notice the feelings you get when you read the following two examples:

- *I want to go to Jamaica. I'd love to feel the white sand sliding between my toes and the warm island breezes caress my face. I can see myself reading*

and sipping fresh coconut juice and jogging along the sleepy shore.
- *I'm so bored in this slow city. I need a vacation. If I drive up the same block one more time and see these same tired faces, I'm going to scream. I've got to get out of here!*

I could literally feel my heart speed up as I wrote the second set of sentences. Often we will feel more like the second example than the first. The second often leads to the first. The second example is where many of us get stuck. We focus on what we dislike instead of appreciating what we want and taking action to make it happen, as in the first example. If we can afford it, we'll plan a trip to Jamaica, buy the ticket, leave, and enjoy ourselves. Many of us have to plan for longer periods of time, save, and jump through many hoops to make it there. Some of us may stop ourselves from imagining all together. Making peace with the present frees your energy to flow toward your desires with excitement and anticipation. By making this peace, you are not running away from, but are embracing the unknown.

Now, don't get me wrong; running away has its place. You may be in a physically or emotionally dangerous situation, or in a situation that is making you ill and you are unable to improve it. I am challenging your habitual way of responding. A good way to gauge yourself is by asking yourself if you are moving toward what you want or away from something that you don't want? If you discover that you are moving away from what you don't want, identify what you do want and focus on how you can obtain it. Focusing on the areas in which you are grateful while acknowledging discomfort can help you to discover your true desires.

What gratitude is not

Gratitude is not synonymous with complacence. You can be grateful and still have desire or ambition. You can desire to travel nationally and internationally. You can want to lose weight; you can want to improve your home, dress, and look and feel better. Being grateful is not an either/or proposition. We think, "If I am truly grateful for who I am and where I am in my life, I wouldn't long to be somewhere else or have what I don't have now." That is not the case.

I tried nagging myself to write, which only worked temporarily. Once I made peace about taking weeks off from writing to renew my mind while completing this book, I could focus on being grateful for the progress I had made. The more I valued and appreciated my efforts, the more I became inspired to write. While typing the manuscript, I imagined how my book could have some impact on the lives of women. I visualized women sharing their stories, becoming motivated to enhance their lives. My positive inner dialogue and images accompanying them fueled my desire to publish this book.

Acknowledging who you are, what you have, and liking the way that you are does not mean you are a slacker and that you do not want more in life. Gratitude means blessing your present circumstances and working in harmony with them, while you simultaneously work to change. You can acknowledge everything that has happened in life. You don't have to like it, but you can be grateful because it has contributed to who you are today.

I'm not telling you to dismiss or deny how you really feel; I just want you to remember to move past that state of mind as quickly as possible. Keeping a gratitude journal and practicing the art of appreciation are tremendous tools that can help in the process.

The more we feed our sense of lack, the more we achieve vibrational harmony with the consciousness of lack. When feelings of scarcity creep into our awareness, it breeds a feeling of disconnection to source. There is no lack in the universe. Abundance abounds. This is the truth, regardless of what the news reports say. As Dr. Wayne Dyer stated, "we don't see situations as they are, we see situations as we are."

The Bible tells us to take out the beam from our eye so that we can see clearly. We interpret our experiences based on the mental stories that we tell ourselves. We get so engrossed in these stories that we become one with them. We reinforce the story with authority and conviction from our ego and view it as fact. Then we begin to act based on the story.

The stories that we tell ourselves can assist us in moving forward or can detour us from our intended destination. When you look into the mirror, what stories are you telling yourself? "I'm getting old. I'm not going to be able to learn how to play the piano at this age." "I have a husband and three kids. I really don't have the time to workout." These are stories. Two important elements of a story are plot and point of view, which you can use to change in your mind anytime you want.

Plot is the action we take or don't take in accordance to our beliefs.. "I can't learn how to play the piano because I'm too old." You tell yourself all types of potentially erroneous stories without questioning them. In situations like this you can ask yourself, "Is what I'm thinking the truth or is it my belief?"

We thicken the plot in our lives when we dare to step out of our comfort zones. The distance between where we are and where we desire to be creates dramatic tension. Obstacles emerge, fear often rears its ugly head, and critical decisions about next steps must be made. Will you create and live your story? Or will you play the role someone else has written for you? Your perspective on what is happening in your life will influence your results.

What perspective are you using when you mentally tell yourself stories? Is it your inner critic? Your Divine voice of wisdom? Your wounded inner child? Pay attention to the perspective from which you are viewing a situation and choose the view that will make you feel the best.

When you are joyful, you have a greater tendency (in the spirit of joy) to give of your time, talent, and money. It is not what you give, but rather the spirit and energy you employ when you give that matters most. Therefore, living with gratitude and giving joyfully of what you can to whom you can opens the way for you to receive more blessings from the universe.

Regular Expression of Gratitude Inspires Joy

Your blessings may not come from the people or sources to which you gave. You will receive good fortune based on the seeds you have sown. Appreciate what you have. Look at nature and all the beauty around you. A feeling of oneness with the universe engulfs you. You see abundance everywhere. Love permeates your being. I feel a sense of oneness when I view excellence in a performance, observe a child adoring his mother, or feasting on a succulent meal. As a work in progress, I'm aiming to nourish my spirit with the feeling of oneness more often.

You become one with infinite intelligence that expands the mind to believe that you can have your piece of the pie. And since the universe is abundant, having your piece of the pie does not detract from another's having her piece of the pie. Seeing abundance and prosperity everywhere expands your consciousness. When your belief in what you can have expands, you can manifest your true heart's desire.

Joy comes from within. Most people believe it's the other way around. They think that they have to do something, buy something, or obtain something before they can be joyful. Having a spirit of gratitude enriches your life even when it is in shambles, or when you're not employed and bills are mounting. In order to work your way out of what you may call negative situations, you have to accept where you are and surrender to your present situation, knowing that it is only temporary. You can live joyfully in spite of the hardships you may be facing by shifting your consciousness to the positive aspects of your life. This is a beginning that should not be underestimated.

In ancient Kemetic tradition, the Goddess of Joy energy is Het-Heru. She is the deity that governs all that is beautiful. According to Ra Un Nefer Amen, the founder and leader of the Ausar Auset Society, her name literally means House (Het) of Heru (the libido, erotic force, sexual vitality that supports the will). In life, this aspect of the Divine is expressed as art, social grace, charm, and peace. The ancient Kemetians acknowledged the various aspects of God and the expressions that took form. So when they saw drawings or sculptures of Het-Heru, their mind was directed to the aspect of God that is gentle, loving, stimulating and holistically pleasure-seeking. These are attributes that you can cultivate within yourself at times of imbalance to help you return to your emotional center.

When the universe appears to go out of its way to challenge us, it is providing feedback on what our conscious and subconscious thought patterns are sending into the ether. It is not about what happens to us, but how we respond to what happens to us that is the real issue. We are spiritual beings on this earthly plane, here to learn and to expand our consciousness. Before you can expand your consciousness, you may need to reframe how you view your past and present circumstances.

Make time for gratitude

There is a better way to live rather than waking up late, gulping down food, hurrying the children off, rushing through the day, attending meetings, attending more meetings, and then falling dead tired into bed. I know many women who look like they "have it all." Many, however, quietly suffer from emotional angst that keeps them going; running from kitchen to committee, from work to school and then to bed, only to have to wake up and start the cycle again in order to prove their worthiness to the world and to themselves. They run to the outside world searching for the magic pill that will bring them the joy that can be found only from within. They run themselves ragged because they have bought into the superwoman myth. They don't take time to nurture themselves, so they grow more resentful toward their responsibilities and others. I should know. I was once that woman!

In many cultures around the world, from ancient Kemet to modern African and Eastern countries, time is perceived as cyclical. There is rebirth, growth, decay, and destruction. Evidence can be seen in nature as well as in myths used to capture concepts and ideas in history and to pass down stories through generations. Time is perceived as linear in the West. One event occurs after another and preceding events influence future outcomes. Thus in the West, our past heavily dictates our future. Here, we have grown accustomed to keeping time, saving time, managing time, being on time, running out of time, wasting time, not having enough time, spending time, giving time, losing time and finding time to have free time or downtime. In essence, there is significant emphasis on controlling our time. Our interpretation of time in the West is often a stress generator. When traveling to countries where the concept of time is more fluid, people are generally more relaxed.

We are most often relaxed when we have downtime. Downtime is when you have nothing on your agenda to do. Your mental and spiritual state during downtime is critical because it is precisely during downtime when people engage in activities that will not lift them up. During "downtime," when no physical actions are needed, thoughts should be turned toward the divine intelligence and carefully monitored. Are you keeping a positive attitude, are you expressing gratitude for your blessings? What are you doing to increase your faith? What you do in your downtime will determine how high you rise because in order to be successful, you must have a constant commitment to success. Not only when you are feeling good, but precisely when you don't feel like it. Remembering your "why" in the midst of your deepest challenges will help you to pull through.

Special internal work should continue in order to generate the energy and magnetic forces needed to attract the right people, situations, money, and material items needed to move you forward. Get beneath the surface and exfoliate the layers of your perceived self in order to uncover the essence of your higher self, which is the storehouse of joy.

Being focused on the abundance already present in our lives leads to the accumulation of good feelings and positive thoughts. Gratitude further produces feelings of joy. You are aligned with the universe going with the flow, not against it. When you are filled with gratitude over what is and what is to be, first acknowledge that the blueprint of your desire already exists on the spiritual plane. Because we are on the physical plane, the densest form of matter, there is a gap between what is created in the spiritual realm versus earthly realm. During the time lag, your job is to continue to think and act in harmony with your intentions in order to match your vibration and your desires. Your thoughts, feelings, actions, and vibration determine your attraction.

Make room for gratitude

Some women have homes that are big, beautiful and a mess. Others have homes that are average-sized, quaint, and still a mess. How we treat the people and things in our environment demonstrate our appreciation of them or lack thereof. Hiring a housekeeper is only part of the solution. Even with hired help, you must have order so that everyone in the household can find what they need when they need it. This orderly environment will minimize everyone's constantly having to ask you where things are.

Many of us long for a bigger house, car, or more material possessions. There is nothing wrong with these desires if we keep in mind that with each new addition comes the responsibility of maintenance. It can be easier to acquire new things than to maintain them. When God's gifts come knocking, will they be able to get in? Or will they have to wait at the door until you create room for them in your mind and environment? All you have to do is take a look inside your closet to answer this question.

Are you among the many women who have a closet full of clothes that you do not wear? Do you keep them in the hope that you will soon lose those extra pounds? Do you keep them just in case you regain those extra pounds? Have you bought items that you weren't particularly fond of just because they were on sale? You can easily spot these clothes because the tags are still on them.

What about that rack of clothes that's too cute to wear? You have to go somewhere special in order to wear them. But you haven't been many places other than work and church.

The clothes are a bit too casual to wear to work and not fancy enough to wear to church. And God forbid that you look that cute walking around the house where no one would see you, except maybe your husband and children. You can't possibly wear these clothes doing mundane things like running to the grocery store or picking the kids up from school. So in the closet they sit.

What are you waiting for? Clean out that closet and wear those nice clothes and take note of how you feel. Not only will the people in your household notice the difference, but you also will feel the difference. Take the time now to free yourself from the excess baggage of clutter. Begin to clear your mind by going on a fast. Remember to start slowly and proceed at a comfortable pace.

Positive information only fast

Be vigilant in protecting what comes into your mind. Hanging around toxic people will drain your life force. In this day and age, it is pertinent that we protect and increase our vitality. We need strength of mind and heart to do the right thing while living our purpose.

In order to be an active participant in life instead of an observer, you must use your will to concentrate your energy toward the fulfillment of your goals. By committing to a 30-day positive-info-only fast, YOU... *WILL DO* the following:

- Read positive literature.
- Engage only in positive conversations.
- Associate with high energy, positive people.
- Commune with nature and breathe in the energy that emanates from God's creation.
- Recite positive affirmations.
- Listen to positive tapes and inspirational videos
- Write notes of appreciation to those who have shown you kindness.
- Forgive someone who has harmed you.

- Forgive yourself for allowing that person to harm you.

YOU WILL NOT:
- Listen to the radio or watch television
- Read the negative information contained online, in newspapers, or in magazines
- Entertain negative thoughts about the past, present, or future

If 30 days is too long, set a time frame that suits your needs.

Go about your day purposefully and full of gratitude. Remember to thank God for being able to read material that will nourish your spirit and inspire you to live your dreams. Praise God for your ability to walk, run, sing, dance, and shout. Thank God for the warm cleansing water that flows freely from the faucet inside your home. Many people around the world still have to walk outside, sometimes miles, for their water. Some have indoor plumbing, but the water may only run cold.

Be still and reflect on the people that God has put in your path to assist you on your journey. I've acknowledged several of my angels at the beginning of this book. Remember to thank God for them all--the good, the bad and the wicked. Each entered your life to teach you a lesson and to heal that part of you that has been wounded. What lessons have you learned from those experiences? Do you look back with regret and in shame or do you look at your past as a stepping stone to a more enriched present and a brighter tomorrow? Did you endure your lessons gracefully, or did you kick, curse, and fight your way through?

Regardless of how you coped with the stress and hardships of your past, you are still here. So take a deep breath and thank God for blessing you with yet another day to reinvent yourself.

Questions for exploration:

Create a list of all the people, things, experiences and situations that you are grateful for. Add to this list in your journal. In what ways do you express gratitude? What does gratitude mean to you?

Affirmations:

- I am grateful for my blessings for they occur at the right time and in divine order.
- I am grateful for my ability to choose how I want to experience my life.
- I am grateful for my body, my mind, and good health.

Action steps:

- Start your day with the intent to find things, people, and situations to appreciate. Look for the lessons and watch your life transform before your eyes.
- Before retiring to bed, make a list of what you are grateful for.
- It's hard to be in a foul mood when you smile. Go forth, smile, and give the sincerest thanks you can give to others. By all means, make sure you thank yourself for taking steps to enhance your life.
- When you receive outstanding service, send a note to the manager or to the headquarters and let the person know that you are doing so.
- Choose to appreciate your present circumstances. Embrace them and thank them for giving you an opportunity to grow and learn.

Application question: In what ways did I express gratitude today?

Secret #2:
Your Inner World Shapes Your Outer World

Your opponent, in the end, is never really the player on the other side of the net, or the swimmer in the next lane, or the team on the other side of the field, or even the bar you must high jump. Your opponent is yourself, your negative internal voices, your level of determination.

—Grace Lichtenstein

Your inner world consists of your thoughts, emotions, and subconscious mind. If you want to move from where you are, let's call this point A, to somewhere else, point B, you can by harmonizing the facets of your inner world. Whether your thoughts, emotions, and subconscious mind are in alignment or not, your outer world will reflect your internal state. Your inner world guides your actions, which then create your circumstances. The good news is that each moment of the day is new and fresh and any time our inner world is not in harmony, we can choose to realign ourselves with our best and highest intentions.

Your inner world of thoughts

Feeding your mind positive, healthy stimuli to affect consciously your thoughts is one of the most important caretaking activities you can do for yourself. Like showering daily, make a habit of consciously feeding your mind by reading uplifting material, listening to motivational CDs and positive music, or spending time in nature. The point is to do whatever uplifts your spirit and rejuvenates your energy. Motivational speaker and author Zig Ziglar says, "Some people say that motivation doesn't last. Well, neither does bathing, that's why you have to do it daily." Weave the practice of nourishing your most precious resource, your mind, into the fabric of your daily life.

If you leave receiving positive stimulation to chance, you may not get the mental nutrients that your mind needs to function at its optimum, joyful level. Not receiving your daily doses of inspiration can make you more vulnerable to being influenced by the negativity of others around you. Chances are slim that you can watch the news all day and constantly talk about how bad things are in the world and still think that you are going to feel good. I'm not advocating putting your head in the sand and ignoring what is going on in the world (although sometimes I recommend it). I am, however, saying that intentional exposure to or consumption of inspiration will counterbalance the negativity in your environment.

Having a positive frame of mind is critical to living a joyful and successful life. Of course, we want to surround ourselves with positive news and people, but sometimes that's not always possible. Therefore, you have to be charged up so that you can remain empowered and energized in spite of what is going on in your environment and in the world.

In spite of our best efforts, we sometimes get depleted and need to take a step back in order to move forward. You needn't feel bad or guilty when you take a respite. It is a nudge from God to love ourselves by resting. If we don't listen to our inner guidance, we become more susceptible to illness, which can creep in and force us to rest. Don't blame God for any unwanted circumstances. He is not punishing and vengeful. God is love and wants us to be happy and prosperous. In Matthew 7:7-8 the Bible states, "Ask, and it shall be given to you; seek, and you shall find; knock and it shall be opened to you. For whoever asks, receives; and he who seeks, finds; and to him who knocks, the door is opened."

To ask means that we first have to get clear about what we desire. Then we have to look for evidence that what we desire is on its way. Keeping our eyes focused on what we want is key at this point. We have to seek, and if we're not finding evidence in our environment, then we have to use our power of imagination and seek it in our mind's eye. To knock means that we have to take action to bring our desires into manifestation. In *Creative Mind and Success* Earnest Holmes says, "Our thought is the seed and mind is the soil. We are always planting and harvesting. All we need to do is to plant only that which we want to harvest." We must pinpoint our desires and focus on them until they are manifested. That does not mean that you have to constantly dig up the seeds to check on their growth. Rather, do the necessary work and water your garden with focused intention and expectancy.

In every goal-oriented motivational book, the author will recommend keeping your goals visible. Some say carry a goal card in your wallet, put it on the bathroom mirror, on the dashboard of your car, or next to your bed so that you can read it every morning. The reason why authors recommend this method is because they know that many people find themselves struggling to focus. Keep your goals and the tracking of your progress in front of you as much as possible. Place them in front of you at work, home, and car where you can easily see them. It's easy for life to take over and to forget what you are supposed to do. With infinite choices at our disposal, executing our purpose and passion in life can get lost in the dance for survival.

If we don't forget about our goals, we tend to send conflicting messages to our minds that are then reinforced by our own actions."I want this. . . but I have no way to get the money." So we have desire, then we stop ourselves before getting starting or quit as soon as the going gets tough. "I would like to learn . . . but it's too late." Almost within the same breath we negate our desires. That is why when we create a hodgepodge of unfinished business that has transformed into a giant monster, we cry, "How on Earth did I get to this point?" Deep inside we know the answer. In James 1:8 the Bible states, "A double-minded man is unstable in all his ways." This is a clear message that emboldens us to stay focused on our desires so that we don't mentally waver and diffuse our energy. Check for energy vampires when you discover misalignments within your inner world.

Energy vampires and what you can do about them

The universe is energy and we all need it to survive and thrive. Anyone or anything that drains your energy and induces a negative feeling state is an energy vampire. Therefore, energy vampires can show up as people, places, things, or even your to-do list.

When a person behaves like an energy vampire, she will say and do things to strengthen her ego, by attempting to usurp your positive energy. They may do this with put-downs, claiming an idea as their own, dominating a conversation, or incessantly proving others wrong.

Sometimes people don't have to steal our energy. Unknowingly, we give it away because we are vulnerable to their vibration when we are not positively charged. I keep myself charged by getting enough rest, praying, exercising, meditating, and repeating my favorite scriptures or poems. Through conscious effort, I have gotten better over the years. By taking care of myself, I'm more aware and not simply existing in a fog where I can be easily blown off course. How do you keep yourself charged? What can you do to increase your own energy?

It is wise to remember that anybody can be an energy vampire, including you. Your negative thoughts are draining to yourself. Over time, they rob you of motivation and joy. By keeping yourself charged up, you can maintain and strengthen your mind. And in turn, you will attract healthy, energetically empowered individuals to you with whom you can engage in mutually positive exchanges that leave all parties uplifted.

The people we see as energy vampires can be viewed as aspects of our higher selves trying to communicate with us. Hip hop star Super Nova Slom, Queen Afua's son, reminded a group of lecture attendees of this viewpoint. He gave an example of a person desiring to start a business. For this person, the thought of being a business owner was exhilarating. This person shared the thought with a close friend. The friend responded by pointing out several reasons why the business would not work.

Nova Slom then asked the group to consider the friend as a projection of ourselves testing how serious and convinced we were about the new business idea. He emphasized that if we held on to our desire, in spite of the reaction of our friend, then we would have passed the test. If we began to doubt ourselves and dismissed the idea then we would have demonstrated to the universe that we were not ready for the opportunity. In essence, our goals and dreams should be protected and nourished until we manifest them.

When I was a sophomore in high school, I wanted to be a physical therapist. I remember sitting in geometry class and doodling because I was clueless about this part of mathematics. I also was feeling particularly discouraged that day because of my dismal test score. As I was walking out the door, I began a conversation with a classmate, and she said that to be a physical therapist, I'd have to take a lot of math. I abandoned my dream of becoming a physical therapist at that very moment. It took years for me to realize that I shouldn't abandon a goal, simply because it is difficult. If I strongly desire to achieve a goal, I now know that I can do it with God and persistent effort.

In graduate school I was tested again. Before relocating to Indianapolis to attend Indiana University-Purdue University at Indianapolis, I decided that I would work full-time and go to school full-time. My peers and some administrators tried to warn me against doing both simultaneously, but I knew that this was the experience that I wanted to have and I did it successfully! My thoughts, emotions, and subconscious mind were in alignment, which helped me manage my circumstances with relative ease.

Our minds focus our attention in certain directions, yet lack of focus or displaced focus can wreak havoc on well-intended plans. Today, take the time to focus on your strengths and visualize future victories. The universe will not know the difference between what is real or imagined and will set into motion events that will recreate whatever is in your mind's eye.

Feng Shui zaps energy vampires

Have you ever been in a place where you could actually feel your energy being zapped? How about being in a place that energizes you? Our physical space plays a subtle and sometimes not so subtle role in affecting our thoughts, emotions, and subconscious mind. The study of how our environment impacts us is the essence of the ancient Chinese practice of Feng Shui. Approximately 6,000 years ago, by studying nature, the Chinese were able to determine the conditions ripe for maximizing experiences. According to Nancilee Wydra, eminent Feng Shui practitioner, "Feng Shui investigates the universal feelings and reactions of human beings to an environment." Essentially, decorating style influences how we experience our environment.

We invest time and money in decorating our homes and constructing work spaces to make them comfortable and easy to inhabit. Although people experience places differently, the artwork, color scheme, furniture style and arrangement, and temperature can make a space warm and inviting or cold and unwelcoming.

You may have experienced walking into someone's home and immediately feeling uncomfortable. This could be for a variety of reasons such as the furniture configuration, extreme order or lack thereof, or even the home's past history. Regardless, something about that space made you feel uneasy. It's always a good idea for new home owners and business owners to bless their new property. Prayer improves the energy of a room.

A space can positively affect you as well. For example, as soon as I enter my friend Anika's home, I feel calm. She plays light jazz in the background. Her attractive art work and incense add to the ambiance and richness of our conversation and tea. The energy inside of her home while relaxing doesn't make me sleepy.

You don't have to worry about falling asleep in office buildings or hotel meeting rooms. The low temperature alone is enough to keep you awake. A prominent office building in downtown Atlanta does not have any seating in the lobby area or outside of the building. It is clear that management does not want people hanging around. They obviously prefer people go directly to the office they intend to visit and leave after they have conducted their business. The historic building is ornate and imposing and is intimidating to many people in the area.

On the other hand, retail businesses and restaurants try to be as welcoming as possible and do their best to make you more receptive to parting with your money. Walk into a spa, restaurant, or department store and you will find all of your senses engaged. You will hear music, see displays, and be invited to taste-test or sample products. Designers know that a familiar color scheme or piece of art work can send your mind strolling down memory lane. The same happens when you smell the aroma of certain foods or recognize a fragrance in the air. Shoppers are impacted greatly by stimuli, which range from subtle to obvious. These stimuli often translate into more dollars for businesses.

Although our inner world shapes our outer world, the science and art of Feng Shui reminds us of how our physical space plays an important role in helping us to function optimally. Our residences and work environments are critically important to our well-being. If we spend so much of our time there, then it is worth the effort to make them work in our favor.

Material things as energy vampires

One of my favorite television shows is Clean House with host Niecy Nash. She and her team makeover cluttered homes. The clutter is so overwhelming for the families that they need expert help. Niecy does an excellent job uncovering root causes of the clutter build-up. The show's guests often have lost loved ones and keep all of their things to cherish their memories. Women have gotten divorced and have lost their will to clean. Guests engage in excessive shopping because of their loneliness. Be aware of the correlations between your environment and your inner world. There is always a reason behind the clutter on the show just as there are reasons for clutter in our own lives.

Not all of us are fortunate to have expert cleaning crews to clear our clutter and redesign our homes. For those of you who have to do it yourselves, the following insights can help you combat energy vampires of material things in your environment.

How do you eat an elephant? Bite by bite. Break large cleaning projects, like basements or garages, into smaller projects and take some time to imagine how good you will feel when you have the order you desire. If the items in your home, such as gifts from past relationships and collector's items that no longer fit your taste, are around your house or in boxes stored in the attic or basement, find them a new home so that you can remove items that no longer fit your lifestyle.

You can use the Star System to do it.

Star System
1. Decide on a goal.
2. Commit to working on that goal for 30 days.
3. Write the goal on a sheet of paper and write the dates for 30 days.
4. Give yourself a star for each day you work toward your goal.

My former colleague, Debbie, is using the Star System to reorganize the closets in her home. She gives herself a star each day she works 15 minutes on her cleaning project. Of course, she regularly ends up working longer. So instead of feeling overwhelmed by this daunting task, she feels relaxed because in her mind cleaning for fifteen minutes is a piece of cake.

Clutter in your home, disorganized closets and drawers, obstructions on the path to your doorway all communicate an outer-world reflection about your internal state. You can see how the material things can become energy vampires if it feels overwhelming.

When you feel your external environment draining your energy, clean it up and remove the energy blockers a bit at a time.

Tame a draining "to-do list"

This potential energy vampire can become one if it is full of tasks that don't reflect your priorities or move you toward accomplishing your goals. When this happens, you are simply doing busy work. In fact, you get so busy checking off tasks that you don't have time or energy to focus on your larger goals. That is why it is essential to break your goals down into manageable pieces and to prioritize them on your to-do list.

When I have over 7 items on my to-do list, I feel my heart race and motivation sink like lead in water. My inner world feels chaotic, so my results reflect what is going on inside. Most times when this happens, it's because I have items on my to-do list that require more steps than I consciously realize, for example: *Notify family members of upcoming celebration.* In order to cross this task off of my list, I will have to do the following:

1. Find out everyone's e-mail address, including those out-of-state.
2. Select a date.

3. Confirm venue.
4. Craft e-mail.
5. Send e-mail with all of the addresses.

Now that I have broken down what needs to be done, I can get help with each item. Mini-projects disguised as tasks on a to-do list go undone and give rise to procrastination, which is draining.

Here are tips for taming your to-do list

1. Make sure items on your to-do list emerge from your priorities.
2. Put tasks on your to-do list, not projects.
3. Carry your list with you and keep it visible.
4. Check off items so that you can feel a sense of accomplishment.
5. Commit to abolishing each task on your list.

In case you are not able to get everything done;

6. Put that item at the top of tomorrow's list.

The inner world of emotions

A pervasive myth exists about the emotional aspect of your inner world. Emotions are psycho-physiological states that move one to action. The myth, according to Dr. Melvyn Kinder, author of *Mastering Your Moods, Recognizing Your Emotional Style and Making it Work for You,* is that "we create what we feel by what we think." While that is partially true, psycho-biologists, who study the biological basis of behavior, have found that the reverse is also true– "emotions can create thoughts." So, the next time you are feeling blue, try changing your physiology, by jumping, skipping, or gushing over something beautiful. The main point is to generate an emotion that will turn your attention to something that feels better to think about.

There is a wonderful song that we sing at church called, "This Joy." And one of the lines goes, "This joy that I have, the world didn't give it to me, the world didn't give it, the world can't take it away." Joy is God-given. And in spite of our circumstances, it is always there, even when we don't feel it. Acknowledging your emotions is a form of self-love that helps you to become more authentic and accepting of yourself. Self-acceptance can help you to achieve the state of happiness and peace that most people seek from the outer world through material things, experiences, and other people. If you find it difficult to accept yourself, then find someone who you admire and emulate their qualities. If they are punctual, giving, or a good listener and you admire those qualities, cultivate them within. By doing your best and feeling good about it, you strengthen your esteem. Material things and people are important, but you can choose not to let them or the lack of them dictate your feelings.

The actions that you take under the influence of your emotions may or may not be in your best interest. Marketers and the media professionals know this; therefore, they do everything they can to influence your emotions so that you will choose their service or product. When your emotions are negatively affected over a period of time, stress is the result. According to the *Merriam-Webster Dictionary*, stress is "a mentally or emotionally disruptive or upsetting condition occurring in response to adverse external influences and capable of affecting physical health, usually characterized by increased heart rate, a rise in blood pressure, muscular tension, irritability, and depression."

A spiritual view of stress is the expression of a personal spiritual crisis. This spiritual crisis occurs on two levels. On one level you are forgetting that you are a spiritual being having a human experience. This means that the real you, your inner divine self that is one with the Creator is the real you. I refer to this as the "the big I in you." If it is true that God is omnipotent, omniscient, and omnipresent, then this means that God is within you and within everything.

The human you is your ego that gets hurt, offended, and experiences the range of emotions that humans have a tendency to experience until you begin to identify with the "Big I" in yourself. Once you remember who you truly are, then you can become an observer of yourself, which gives you the distance necessary to respond by choice. Then you can remember that:

- Challenges are opportunities for spiritual growth.
- You are a spiritual being having a human experience.
- You can choose to respond differently to events and circumstances.
- Your habits have gotten you where you are today, and if you change your habits, you will change your life.

When I was a senior in college, I took my first yoga class. The eight-week session was taught by a professor who co-owned with his wife a cultural center and African-American bookstore. Many of the students that I met at the center were vegetarians. Although I didn't grow up eating pork, it was hard to conceive of not eating meat, especially chicken. I shifted back and forth between eating meat and not eating meat for many years. Once I learned to make delicious tofu and other vegetarian meals, and discovered vegetarian options at restaurants, the habit of vegetarianism was easier to incorporate as a lifestyle.

We can use our will to overcome our conditionings like drinking fewer sugary drinks or choosing to be at peace when experiencing perceived slights, hurts, or injustices. Choosing to be at peace is not synonymous with inaction or not addressing issues. Challenges are ripe opportunities to exercise our spiritual muscles that must be used in order to make changes in our lives.

When you find yourself flying off of the handle, ask yourself why a particular response or action from someone else bothered you, and get to the root of the issue. Honesty with yourself will reveal what needs to be healed on the inside, in order to change your perception of or eliminate undesirable conditions on the outside. This approach is very important because each time a person says something to you that you don't like, you are going to react in the same way until you become conscious and choose to react differently or deal with the underlying issue so that you are no longer bothered by certain actions.

Managing your emotions

In order to manage your emotions, you have to exercise your will. According to Ra Un Nefer Amen, a leading authority on ancient Egypt (Kemet) and founder of the Ausar Auset Society, "The main reason that your emotions fluctuate so drastically is because you are not in the habit of maintaining peace in the midst of a challenge." This is easier said than done. We often simply revert to our habitual emotional responses when challenges, which are spiritual growth opportunities, arise. Prayer, meditation, and other centering spiritual practices are preparation for the times when we have to face our various challenges in life. Your spiritual practice helps to increase your faith, gives you more confidence, and ultimately helps you to navigate life.

Love and fear are the primary emotions from which all other emotions spring. Love and fear are the opposites of the same coin, yet they interact to produce situations that are ripe for our spiritual growth and learning. FEAR (False Evidence Appearing Real) has many guises and will cause you to do some very strange things.

I know you may not indulge in petty trifles, but we all know "other people" who do. Fear will make you tell small and sometimes big, white lies. It will make you backbite. It will make you undermine friends and colleagues. It will twist your tongue and make you mute when you need to be heard. It will make you spill your guts when silence should reign supreme.

An action based on fear comes from an innate primitive instinct that keeps us from harm or from experiencing too much pain. You must understand, however, that situations that evoke powerful emotions should stimulate exploration into deeper parts of the self. They invoke a response from our inner animal, the undisciplined part of the self that is conditioned by our ego and environment.

When you find yourself in a situation that sparks a reaction from your lower self, stop and breathe. Breathe in the essence of life and decide that you are not going to allow this person or situation to move you from your center. It is imperative that you decide because it is easy to allow outside stimuli to dictate your mood or behavior.

Emotions play a role in life (letting you know that you are at a crossroads for a spiritual test), but as the master, you decide what role they will play. Just as dog owners send their beloved pet to doggy daycare for training and companionship, you can do the same to your inner animal. Put it on a spiritual leash and let it know that you will be in charge from here on.

Start by acknowledging its existence. Second, embrace it. Next, retrain it by choosing a different response. Associate with positive others for motivation. Learn about the best practices for handling various situations. Lastly, celebrate each small victory. I used this process to publish this book.

Whenever you start a new endeavor, it's easy to hit the ground running. But what happens when the motivation and enthusiasm dissipates? How do you move forward in spite of the challenges ahead? When writing this book, I had to acknowledge that sometimes I didn't have the discipline or motivation to sit and write. I would find any reason to procrastinate. Once I acknowledged that I needed a break from writing, I felt relieved and was able to enjoy fully my other activities without thinking that I should be writing. I embraced the fact that I needed time away from the book. After a while, however, my breaks became longer and longer. I found myself going months without looking at my manuscript. I had other friends who were also in the process of writing books, so we actively encouraged one another at various times. Writing a book can be a deeply personal and solitary endeavor. My habit of undisciplined writing was a barrier to my finishing this book. I knew that I would have to develop discipline in this area in order to grow personally and professionally.

The desire to complete the manuscript became so strong that I made a decision to become a more disciplined writer. I had to make that decision; otherwise, I would have never completed this book. Besides, I read about the writing process from other successful authors and they all say the same thing. You have to sit down and write. There is no way around this unless, of course, you have a ghost writer.

Once I began eating a raw vegan diet, my energy skyrocketed and my focus improved. I became more disciplined in my writing. My new level of energy eradicated excuses about being tired. I began celebrating small victories by rewarding myself in various ways like buying ingredients for a special new recipe, or watching my favorite television shows like *Oprah*, *The Baby Story*, and *Bringing Baby Home*. I had delicious treats that kept me motivated to write. The ecstatic feeling of completing a writing session soon became reward in itself; my treats were an added bonus.

Writing this book was a lengthy process of managing my emotions. Nevertheless, the process is applicable to almost any situation regardless of the annoyance. For example, when someone cuts you off in traffic, instead of giving her the finger or honking your horn ballistically, breathe and be grateful that everyone is safe. When you are communicating with others, decide to communicate from the wellspring of love instead of from the dark moat of fear. Know that actions sometimes fall short of our ideals. The beauty is in the growth that we experience from maintaining the will to love what we are doing.

Your feelings alert you to your thoughts. When you are feeling down or just downright negative, your mind scans your internal and external environment to generate thoughts that will align with the negative emotion. The same is true for positive emotions. No matter what we are feeling in a particular moment, acknowledging how we feel and accepting the emotion leads to greater authenticity. It is not what happens *to* you, it's how you respond to what happens that demonstrates your growth.

The subconscious mind

The inner world of your subconscious mind also shapes your external experiences. So the program currently installed in your subconscious mind has taken you to where you are today. If you want a major change in your life or you want to move from point A to point B, then reprogramming your subconscious mind will assist you. The subconscious mind stores images, beliefs, and other latent mental constructs, which aid what is manifested in your outer world. Your conscious mind filters and objects while your subconscious mind simply accepts and carries out the commands of the conscious mind. It is the duty of your conscious mind to play this discriminatory role so that it can help you to discern and make choices in life.

What we see affects our subconscious mind as much as what we hear. Sight can be divided into two main areas, internal and external imagery, yet they both come from within. Internal images are formed from the pictures we create in our mind from our imagination or from our external environment. External images also derive from our imagination.

Internal images can come from our imagination or they can be recreated from something that we have seen or experienced in our waking state. These images are imprinted into our subconscious mind and affect our behavior by embedding themselves into our cellular memory. So, the plethora of our experiences imprinted on a cellular level help to form the physiological basis for habitual stimulus and response. The use of internal imagery is a powerful programming tool. With your conscious awareness, you can create what you imagine. It may not come to pass exactly when you want, but if your deep desires remain consistent and you work toward the goal, when you look up, you'll often find yourself where you wanted to be. When used as intended, internal and external sight can instill or reinforce positive beliefs and expectations. Creating a vision board by drawing and cutting out pictures of your desires is a wonderful example of how your subconscious mind can be subtly persuaded to accept the vision you create on your board as reality.

From time immemorial, words, sounds and music have been used as tools for transformation. Words are generally associated with our conscious mind as expressed by the common saying, "Be conscious of the words you speak." There is another element of words, however, that produces change on a metaphysical level in our lives.

Ted Andrews, the author of *Sacred Sounds*, explains in his book how language affects us on a cellular level. He says, "Every cell within our body is a sound resonator...muscular actions can be altered, strengthened or balanced through the use of sound." The intent behind our words and the tonality of our voices create vibratory frequencies. These resonate and affect our subconscious mind which becomes the point of our attraction. These sounds bypass our critical mental faculty and affect us on the physical and astral planes. That's why repeating a mantra such as "OM" is powerful. The sound creates harmony and balances energy in the body. On an astral level, we have an energetic field that surrounds our body, which many refer to as our auoric field or aura. Therefore, when healing takes place, it must take place on the energetic or astral level and at the physical level. The mind is also transformed in the process.

In Masaru Emoto's book *The True Power of Water*, he shows us the effect of our thoughts and words on water crystals. On various water bottles were written words, like "good job," "easygoing," and "stupid." The water in the bottles with the words "good job" and "easygoing" transformed into beautiful whole crystals, while the water with the word "stupid" on it looked murky and failed to fully form a crystal shape. If thinking and speaking disempowering words has this effect on water, and we are composed of seventy percent water, imagine the damage we can do to ourselves. Or imagine the enormous power we have to maximize our healing potential.

Music has a similar effect on the subconscious mind because of the vibrations that are produced. Watching television or listening to certain kinds of music or songs can put you in a suggestive state. So what you are hearing and not hearing is being implanted in your subconscious mind. The information lies dormant until a trigger is activated. Everyone has a different trigger, whether it is emotional, physical, or psychological. Just like words, music can be used as a powerful healing tool that bypasses our critical mental faculties and directly impacts our emotions.

Use the following techniques to change your thoughts, manage your emotions, and re-program your subconscious mind.

Change your thoughts:
- Focus on what you desire to experience instead of what you don't want to experience.

Manage your emotions:
- Create a mental touchstone that you will revisit anytime you feel the need to change your mood. A touchstone can be something physical or even a positive memory that you think about in order to shift your attention to something more pleasurable. Make your touchstone something that will make you smile when you think about it. You may need several touchstones according to the severity of the situation and your mood. Sometimes listening to music may help. When it doesn't, have something else that can soothe your spirit like going for a walk or reading. Use these touchstones as ways to focus and shift your flow of energy. Revisit your discord when you are less emotionally charged and have clearer thoughts.

Reprogram your subconscious mind:
Slowly count backward from fifty while you concentrate on breathing deeply. Once you get to five, state your desire affirmatively out loud or to yourself, then visualize it in detail. Do this for twenty-one days: first thing in the morning and before going to bed each night.

Questions for exploration:
- List examples of past successes and why you consider them successes.
- From the above list, what were your dominant thoughts at that time?
- What qualities did you exhibit to help you achieve success in the examples above?

Affirmations:
- I am determined to put forth the effort and energy required to achieve my goals.
- I have made a decision to succeed and I know what success looks like and feels like to me.
- I use my inner strength at the right time and in the right places.

Action steps:
1. Find people who exhibit qualities that you admire and observe them. Ask if you can set up a time to have lunch and ask for their advice in areas where you may need a boost.
2. Make a decision to continue striving for your goals no matter what the circumstances are.
3. For those of you who like deadlines, give yourself one. Say that you will complete _____ in _____ days/weeks/months.
4. Read books about people who have persisted in their goals.
5. Do a little bit each day, even if it's simply thinking, talking, or visualizing your desires.

Application Question:
What are you determined to accomplish within a year? month? week?

Secret #3:
Your Mood is a Habit

Our ultimate freedom is the right and power to decide how anybody or anything outside ourselves will affect us.
—**Steven Covey**

Your mood is a temporary state of mind based on your feelings. The operative word here is temporary. The fleeting nature of moods allows us to be resilient and in touch with our feelings, which are caused by chemical reactions in our brains. These reactions make us have pleasant, unpleasant, or neutral feelings.

Our feelings are intensified or deepened based upon how we think about the way we feel. For example, if you feel angry, what's most important is not only how you deal with your anger, but what you think about being angry. If you think that being angry is somehow inferior, negative, or unspiritual, you will add feelings of guilt to your anger because of your belief. Our responses over the years to various stimuli have become engrained patterns. Therefore our sustained habitual, responses turn our moods into a habit.

Using the mood as habit framework, we can retrain ourselves to experience better moods more of the time through what I call DEPTH—how we Do, Eat, Pray, Think and Have. We will explore each element and share ways you can use them to create more pleasurable moods in your life.

D is for Do

When you create your to-do list, do you secretly begrudge it? Is it a list that you feel you "have" to complete? Or do you approach your to-do list with the anticipation and excitement that you will successfully handle your business for the day? You can enhance the joy in the process of getting things done when you are confident that you are doing your best. You can measure how well you are doing by monitoring how present you are in the moment, how involved you are in what is going on around you, and how engaged you are in activities in your life.

Acknowledging your feelings allows you to enjoy life with all of its twists and turns. Eckert Tolle, in the groundbreaking book, *The Power of Now*, talks about the power of being in the present. Being able to focus and harness your energy is powerful. Being present is only the first step. To get more out of life, you have to do more than just be present, you have to get involved. Involvement, in this sense, means that you are actively participating in life. Not just on the sidelines, nor do you just show up. But ultimately, you want to be engaged. At this level you are taking charge of your life, being responsible for the vibrations that you send out, owning your issues, and making a conscious effort to work through them. So life's enjoyment comes from what you do and, more importantly, how you do it.

E is for Eat

We spend a significant amount of time eating. Although what we eat is vitally important to the proper functioning of our bodies and minds, we need to pay increased attention to how we eat. Food provides nourishment for the body, mind, and soul. Religions throughout the ages have incorporated the sanctity of eating or fasting for physical and spiritual purposes.

According to Deborah Kesten, author of *Feeding the Body, Nourishing the Soul*, "Turning toward food for spiritual sustenance is a universal concept that has journeyed through the centuries, appearing today in every culture and religion throughout the world." When we are spiritually empty, we have a tendency to eat more. We use food to fill a void that can only be filled by a personal relationship with God. That relationship transforms our kitchen consciousness as well. When we feel connected with our higher power and prepare food with love for those we are serving, even when it is for ourselves, our food becomes more than just something to satisfy our hunger; it nourishes our spirit as well. Scarfing down food or eating on the run in our cars disconnects us from the sacredness of this holy act.

We have all heard or perhaps even experienced our grandmothers or mothers preparing food that appeared not to be enough to fill everyone. Yet, somehow it was always enough. My Aunt Helen and Uncle Pumpkin live in Jackson, Tennessee. Our family and extended family members living predominantly in Milwaukee could visit anytime. Aunt Helen and Uncle Pumpkin are filled with so much love that their home, when I was growing up, was always filled with family and friends sharing laughter and food. We would sit around the table for hours eating and enjoying each other's company. We savored the meal, stopping often to praise the cook, my Aunt Helen or Uncle Pumpkin. The food that I ate when visiting, besides being downright delicious, filled me with a happiness that I experience all over again whenever I think about it.

Our busy lives aren't always conducive to keeping an elevated consciousness in the kitchen. When we bring our full attention to preparing and consuming food, we reawaken to our connection with the source of all things. Eating with this awareness alone can have a grounding effect. If we are feeling spacey and need to re-center ourselves, this connection puts us on the path to improving our mood.

P is for Prayer

How you pray is about the spirit in which you pray. Are you merely repeating words, or do you put energy behind your words? Are you asking for a greater consciousness of God or is your main focus on acquiring new things? These questions assume the traditional view of prayer. One Sunday morning my husband and I visited a Unity church in Washington D.C. The congregation sang a powerful song called *Our Thoughts Are Prayers*. Hearing it nearly brought tears to my eyes.

> Our thoughts are prayers,
> and we are always praying.
> Our thoughts are prayers,
> take charge of what you're saying.
> Seek a higher consciousness,
> a state of peacefulness.
> And know that God is always there,
> and every thought becomes a prayer.

"Our thoughts are prayers and we are always praying." What an enlightening way to think about the sacred power of our thoughts. If you are always praying, then ask yourself, what are you praying for? When you think thoughts of sickness, subconsciously, you're praying for sickness. When you think thoughts of being broke, you're praying for scarcity. When you think thoughts of tiredness, you're praying for lethargy. Or when you think all three, you're saying, "I'm sick and tired of being broke!" and you attract more of the same into your life. Earnest Holmes sums it up perfectly in his book *Creative Mind and Success*. He says, "You will find that you are surrounded by a Mind, or Law, that casts back at the thinker, manifested, everything that he thinks." So, think only about what you want in your life. Do not think in terms of what you don't want.

"Our thoughts are prayers, take charge of what you're saying." Not only do we affect others with our words, but more importantly, we create an aura around us that attracts and repels according to our subconscious thoughts, words, and actions. We can use our words to uplift or destroy. Hurt or heal. Encourage or disparage. When we take charge and improve the quality of our thoughts, it will manifest in what we say and do.

"Seek a higher consciousness, a state of peacefulness." On every envelope and letter my mother writes me, to this day, she adds, "keep striving to keep God 1st." In essence, she is telling me to seek a higher consciousness in everything that I think and do. We can seek a higher consciousness by going to that quiet place within and declaring our intention for wisdom, understanding, and peace. We can tap into that universal source and emerge renewed and feeling powerful and peaceful.

"And know that God is always there and every thought becomes a prayer." By continuously cultivating our spirits, we will feel the presence of God anchored within and all around us. And when we think and believe this to be so, everything we think, say, and do will become a prayer. So we are, in fact, praying without ceasing. Our responsibility is to grow more conscious of our thoughts or what we are praying for in our lives.

T is for Think

As a professor, my husband has a flexible schedule. He lovingly prepares my lunch for work each day. He places my food in various containers. Sometimes I eat all of my food, other times I don't. Because I don't have a garbage disposal at work, I was in the habit of leaving the food in the containers until I arrived home. You can imagine how much more difficult it was to wash the containers after having food in them for hours. It didn't make preparing my lunch that evening fun when he first had to spend time scrubbing out the containers.

Because my husband washes the dinner dishes, he would also wash the containers. Since I enjoyed the privilege of having my breakfast and lunch prepared for me daily, I figured the least I could do is to make it easier for him. So I decided to change my habit from leaving food scraps in my containers to washing the containers before arriving home. The first day I brought home clean containers, my husband was so happy. This small gesture was a major deal in our household.

One day, as I was washing my containers at work, I realized that I wasn't just washing dishes, I was creating more peace, love, and harmony in my marriage. When I woke up to this realization, it changed how I began to look at everything.

A similar challenge arose when I was suddenly required to attend a training session at work. Under normal circumstances I would have loved to go. This was a last-minute training opportunity that required me to be out of the office all day. My first reaction was that I would be present at the training, but not engaged. I had planned to sit in the back and think about and do other things. Then I remembered how that was my conditioned response. This time, I decided to respond differently. I asked myself, how can I motivate myself to attend this all-day class? Since the class was on budgeting for nonprofits, and I desired to have my own business, why not pay attention and learn something, not only for my business but to enhance my knowledge and skills in this area? Once I reframed my thoughts about the training, I was able to be both present and engaged.

Consider how reframing your thoughts can improve your present circumstances. By seeing the growth opportunities latent within each situation you face, you can respond in a way that maximizes your personal growth.

H is for Have

There is a difference between having what you need and having what you want. Abraham Maslow, American psychologist and father of humanistic psychology, laid a firm foundation categorizing human needs. Based on Maslow's hierarchy of needs theory, once your survival and safety and physiological needs are met, you're moved to obtain social needs of friendships and supportive family. All of the these needs are considered deficiency needs, which means that it is critical for them to be met in order to move to higher levels on the pyramid. Once these basic needs are met, the more you acquire won't necessarily add to your happiness.

The more we become attached to things and people in our lives the more likely we will be disturbed if these things or people are lost or taken away from us. When those that we love get hurt or transition into another realm, it is normal to feel pain or sorrow. When divorce happens or a friendship ends, healing needs to occur. My main concern here is with unhealthy attachments to people and things. Our attachments become problematic when they threaten our well-being.

The key is to need less while keeping your wants high. This combination is a recipe for motivation that will keep you striving, not from a sense of lack, but from the desire to have various experiences in order to be of greater service to others. When we create from this position, we are better able to release and share our resources that in turn improve our esteem and our mood. Once your basic needs are met, you can focus on obtaining more of what you want.

Mood recognition takes awareness

I like to wake up in the morning determined to be optimistic and outgoing, and not to have a vendetta against the world for whatever reason. This hasn't always been the case. Sometimes I still struggle. Do you ever wonder why you feel good and then when you leave a certain environment, you start feeling badly? Early on in my relationship with my husband, we noticed that we would somehow manage to get ourselves into a minor conflict on Sunday evenings.

Just when it began to get dark, around 6 p.m., we would get agitated. Finally, we noticed a pattern. Sunday evenings, for us, signaled the end of a joyous weekend. It was the official beginning of the work week. In order to change our pattern, we made Sunday evenings a time when we would do our spiritual work. During this time, we would focus on what we were grateful for, we would pour libation to honor our ancestors, and we would dance and sing together. Suddenly we began to look forward to our Sunday evening rituals. Not long after we implemented the new plan, the Sunday evening irritations disappeared. We implemented strategies to enhance our moods. We were better able to choose our mood, before it had a chance to choose us.

Many people get confused and think that feeling good just happens. You have to learn to be proactive so that you can create the environment and feelings that you want. Whether we want to or not, we need to understand that how we feel is ultimately up to us.

Out of everything in the world, the one thing that you do have control over is your mind and how you choose to think and feel. You must decide that you want to be optimistic and simply joyful. As easy as this may sound, many of us fail to make that choice. Instead we simply leave our feelings to what is happening in our environment. If you are not proactive in choosing your mood, you will be susceptible to the moods of others, as well as to external stimuli. Mood is energy that is in constant motion, changing and shifting from one state to another.

To illustrate, I sometimes get so focused during a project that I begin to neglect the spiritual and emotional significance of what I am doing. For example, I was working on a calendar to commemorate our annual Robertson Family Day Celebration. Twice, when I was nearly done with the calendar, it was erased. Each time it happened, however, I discovered a better way to do it. Finally, when I was ready to submit my order, I experienced severe computer glitches. The glitches required me to redo some parts of the calendar, and mistakes showed up. Of course, after feeling a bit frustrated, yet realizing that each problem was really a benefit, I had to slow down and breathe. Each time I had become so focused on completing the calendar, I did not set my intention, nor ask for divine guidance. I thought this was going to be a simple no-brainer task that actually turned out to be more complicated than I had anticipated. My mood swayed in harmony with the flow of my family calendar project. As soon as I relaxed and summoned spirit, I was able to complete the project.

Your mood as a habit is a secret because you are conditioned to believe that you have to respond in a certain way based on external stimuli. For example, if someone offends you, your mood is usually negatively affected. Even though you may not show it, you talk to others about how you cannot believe what "so-and-so" said. It may burn you up inside sometimes for days, weeks, and even years. When someone says something that is offensive, you must understand that the feelings elicited are only signals. Check out what is going on in that particular area of your life that has caused you to choose to be offended rather than at peace.

Hetep is a state of peace in Kemetic tradition that represents the peace that we desire to maintain. Do we want to live in a state of confusion, anger, and depression? Or do we want to live with joy and a peaceful heart? It is my assumption that if you are reading this book that you strongly desire to experience the peace that being joyful has to offer. Being here on Earth gives us unlimited reflections of possibilities. We have the opportunity to see neutral events as either positive or negative. Because we judge constantly, we color and cannot accept what is. It is important for us to allow others to be who they are, while we are who we are. There are always two sides of every coin. They are there whether we choose to focus on them or not. Where we put our focus will often determine our thoughts, which in turn affects our moods.

In Kemetic philosophy there is an energy called Nekhebet. Nekhebet and Uatchet are receptive and dominant energies, respectively, that influence subtle bodies that exist within you. If you have more Nekhebet energy, you have the tendency to be influenced by other stronger personalities, mass media, suggestion, and other subtle forces. Writer and author Martha Beck calls it "being spongy," where you more easily absorb the energy of those around you. If you have more Uajet energy, you are the one you exert greater influence on your environment and on others around you. You set the tone.

Being aware that these types of energies exist will increase your capability to recognize the effect they could possibly have on you, if you allow them to flow freely. Staying conscious throughout your day is very important. The more conscious you are, the better. Please do not fall into the trap that some people will set by saying that you have to be willing to go with the flow. You can go with the flow if you want to, but you had better choose where and how you want to flow. There are many different streams of thought that exist out there. I don't have a problem with going with the flow, if the flow means flowing in the direction where I want to go.

Advertisers spend billions of dollars to influence you to think in a way that will increase your desire for their products or services. People want you to act in ways that benefit them. Everyone has her own agenda. Isn't it time for you to take control and create an agenda for yourself? Decide how you want to feel. Then set out to live your day in that state, for as long as you can. Deciding how you want to feel some of the time is better than spending most of your days frustrated, bitter, and cynical about the choices you have made and the consequences of such decisions.

How can you put this type of consciousness into action? Jerry and Esther Hicks talk about the concept of prepaving. Prepaving is the psychic way of preparing to receive an experience. You visualize what you want to happen, see it in detail and then act according to how you wish to experience your reality. The experience is first created mentally and then it is sent out into the universe.

Prepaving, like visualizing, gives you the space and time needed to bring a desire or goal into manifestation. It allows you to release the mental and spiritual energies to work for you in the etheric realm so you can focus your physical energies on the goals at hand. It also gives your mind the time needed for expanded ideas to take root in your subconscious. It's as if the ideas are germinating seeds, waiting for the appropriate moment to come to fruition.

It takes time for your mind to adjust to your new level of thinking and being. But it will only take as long as your mind accepts that it will take. This is why visualizing your new self is so important. A miracle happens when our results exceed what we thought was possible. Transformations occur when we have a paradigm shift in our thinking from one way to another. Transformations can be instantaneous, or they can take years and years depending on your level of consciousness.

I found prepaving to be the most useful when preparing for future events. One of my professional development goals was to join a grant review committee to read proposals. Working on the committee would help me understand how and why some proposals are declined and others are funded. Although I didn't write it down at the bottom, of my to-do list, it was imprinted on my mind for a year. Once the goal became an official part of my professional development plan and written down, I knew I was going to accomplish it. At the time I didn't know how I was going to achieve this goal, but I knew that I would. One week later, a friend sent an e-mail asking if anyone wanted to join a committee to review proposals for a federal grant.

Here is the prepaving process. Make your to-do list, whether you write it daily or weekly. At the end of the to-do list, write "prepave" and underneath write down all the things that you wish to see happen. Then go about your business as usual, while you leave the items underneath the prepave section to God. Know within your heart that these manifestations are coming to pass and you are being prepared to receive them when the time is right.

Read your prepaved list daily, but do not do anything. Remember, in the early stages, no action is required. Simply let the universe work on your behalf. Soon you will feel ready to take steps toward that which you have prepaved. You can put items that were once on your prepaved list onto your to-do list. By following this order, your steps will be fully integrated into your spirit and desires. You will no longer have a conflict within yourself that inhibits its manifestation.

It is also most useful when you have a full agenda. Let's say that you're working on several projects. With prepaving, you leave room and mental space to focus on the tasks at hand while holding on and clearly visualizing what it is that you want to manifest. If your visualizations are vivid, you can have your cake and eat it too. Your spiritual helpers are diligently working in the inner planes, preparing the hearts and minds of others to give you what you seek. Prepaving puts you in a positive frame of mind as you think about your desires. In essence, you are being prepared through the conditioning of your mind and heart to receive your good.

One way to visualize the details of what you want to manifest is through daydreaming. This isn't just for children. Daydreaming is a very useful exercise to prepare yourself to fulfill your desire. Take time to daydream. Daydreaming about something good will inspire you and put you in a better mood. It costs nothing. There are no risks involved, and your body chemistry does not really know the difference between an imagined experience and a real one. When you daydream, see things the way you want to see them. Why imagine the worst when you have total control over the picture you see in your mind's eye? A great question to ask yourself is, what would the ideal situation look like? Notice the question is self-directed. This is an important distinction because often, even in the world of our own thoughts, we worry about what other people are thinking, instead of what we want.

Another way to prepave is though meditation. Now I know many of you are used to meditation as being a time to listen to your higher inner voice. Meditation can also be used to visualize what you want. This is the time where you can see yourself tapping into the joy that you wish to experience in more of your life. During meditation you can inhale or breathe in your desires and exhale the habits you want to eliminate. After the first few minutes, focus only on what you want. Spending too much time thinking about what you do or do not want confuses the brain. Therefore, it is recommended that you only think about what you want.

It is amazing to see many situations turn out almost exactly as I envision them. When my visions do not materialize, I know there is good reason, and I am more prepared mentally and emotionally to handle the situations with equanimity. This state

Your Mood is a Habit

of mind has allowed me and many other women to be joyful in times where we could surely choose to be otherwise.

Muslims are required to pray five times a day; this is a time to reflect and praise God. People often go through the day without reflecting on the various experiences that we have. A quick reflection is all that is needed to recognize when we feel an energy shift. When I followed this prayer ritual, I noticed a significant increase in my consciousness, my patience increased, and I was much more focused. It was a challenge to meet the five obligatory prayers each day. My schedule alone was a hardship. I remember one year while in college I was on Ramadan, the Muslim time of fast. Muslims are also supposed to read the *Quran* in its entirety.

One evening I was faced with the dilemma either to read my allotted portion of the *Quran* or to study for my biology exam. I opted to read my portion of the *Quran* and did not have time to study for the exam. When I got to the exam, I felt that if I had studied the evening before, I would have done much better. That evening, once again, I was presented with the option to read my portion of the Quran or to study for another exam. I opted to study for the exam. I walked into the classroom the next morning feeling confident and prepared. I had kept up my studies all semester and my study session the night before solidified my prospect of earning a very good grade. When I received the results of my exams, I earned an A- on the first test and a C^+ on the second test. I couldn't believe it. That lesson, to put God first, will always stick in my mind.

Joyfulness is a sense of deep gratitude that lasts and is embedded in the foundation of who you are. It penetrates deeper than the sorrows that wound the soul. Sometimes it means accepting what you cannot change while changing what you can.

Please understand that it is okay for you to be in a foul mood. It happens to all of us. The best thing about feeling off-centered is the opportunity for growth. You can explore the feeling and get to the root of the issue. Also, you do not have to react based on your mood, although it is very human to do so.

There is a distinct difference between reacting and responding. When you react, you act based on conditionings, habitual behaviors learned during childhood.

It is important to honor all of your feelings. Allow them to have access to you. Do not repress or deny them. They are there for you to acknowledge and transmute. They have a distinct purpose; you have to own them. This does not mean that you have to hold the feelings tight. They are to help you to grow. Determining what to do is an important step in the process of transmuting the negative energy generated by lower vibration feelings.

Acknowledging your deepest feelings to yourself is a powerful elixir to help your joy return, especially when you give yourself time to feel what you are feeling. You can decide how long to feel that way, but then ask yourself how to improve the situation. What can you do to make the situation work out for the best? Ask yourself questions that will stimulate you to think about remedies instead of dwelling on the negative feeling.

Another acronym that I like to work with is my name. ASIA equals Ask, State Intentions and then Act. Many people have it the other way around. They act, then decide what they want based on the results that they get, and then sometimes they ask for divine assistance to get them out of the mess they've created.

The complex web of life presents a number of opportunities to collect data on what you want in your life. If you have feelings of jealousy, that is your spirit longing for you to manifest more in your life in your life. Often when we have these feelings, we beat ourselves up for having them, try to ignore them, or push them aside because we are conditioned to believe that they are bad or negative. If we act based on these feelings, we can enter cycles of self-doubt and tough love.

If you are constantly feeling as though you are not in the present moment then you need to look deeper within yourself to find out why. What is the root cause of the ache in your heart

Your Mood is a Habit

that you experience so much of the time? Then ask yourself what small step you can take to make a change?

When you spend the weekend struggling to gear up for the coming week, you know that it is time to make a change in what you are doing throughout the week. This doesn't necessarily equate to leaving your job. It may mean performing a different job in the same workplace. It may mean cutting back your hours. It may mean leaving. Whatever the case may be, you must be willing to let go and let God, which means that you will have to exercise faith and trust in your indwelling intelligence.

A major part of choosing your mood is choosing how and when to recharge your battery. The key to this timing is finding what works for you. If meditation works, that is great. If going for a swim or a long walk works, then that's great too. Recharging your battery allows you to restore your energy. It gives you an opportunity to refocus on what is important and to better monitor your own feelings, actions and responses.

Many women are frazzled. They are too busy to take care of themselves or to notice they are, in fact, stressed. It sneaks up on them and pounces like a hungry lion. If you are around a stressed-out person, you know that person can "bite your head off" for little or no reason. When we act out, it's because we're what I describe as SHOT: Sleepy, Hungry, Offended, or Tired.

Rejuvenation is the key to staying balanced, or at least sane, in the world of business. Choosing your mood is a wonderful demonstration of your power. Acknowledge and affirm your feelings, then choose your mood. When you make decisions that are in your best interest so that you can better care for family and those you love, you are using God's divine laws properly, which has a healing effect on your spirit. When you have to will yourself to feel joyful, know that you do have a choice. And declare that nothing will disturb the peace of your soul. Then go about and act accordingly. Now you are communicating energetically that you care enough to set boundaries and that you love and care for yourself.

Questions for exploration:
- What decisions have made you feel exceptionally proud?
- How did you feel when you made those decisions?
- What choices do you need to make in order to bring out more joy in your life?

Affirmations:
- I am calm and nothing can disturb the calm peace of my soul.
- I consciously choose how I will respond to situations and in this moment I choose peace.
- Mother, Father God, help me in this situation so that I may respond from my highest Self.

Action steps:
- Today, choose to be deliberate about what you do. Just because your co-workers bring sugary snacks and leave them on the table for everyone to enjoy doesn't mean that you have to eat them too... at least, not immediately. If you are compelled to indulge, take the snack and save it for later. If you're feeling really empowered, forego the treat and choose a healthy alternative.
- Clean out your closet and choose to keep all the clothes that make you feel and look great. Give the rest to charity.
- The next time you are talking to someone and you don't agree with what she says, choose to express your opinion. Know that your opinion is fine, simply because it is yours.
- Play the devil's advocate. Instead of speaking from your viewpoint, see the situation from multiple perspectives and express your thoughts.

- Choose one thing that you do not like to do. Try to figure out the source of this aversion. Do not spend too much time here. Instead, come up with ways to make the experience more enjoyable. Perhaps playing music while you do it. Do it in candlelight while sipping a cup of chamomile tea. Think about how you will feel after it has been completed. Be creative. Before you know it, you may just start looking forward to doing whatever it is!

Application question:
- Did you have to consciously choose your mood today? If so, what did you say to yourself or do to choose?

Secret #4:
You are the Center of Your Universe

The tragedy in life doesn't lie in not reaching your goal. The tragedy lies in having no goal to reach. It isn't a calamity to die with dreams unfulfilled, but it is certainly a calamity not to dream. It is not a disaster to be unable to capture your ideal, but it is a disaster to have no ideal to capture.
—**Benjamin E. Mays**

While growing up you may have heard statements like, "the universe doesn't revolve around you" or "you're acting like you're the center of the universe." I'm here to remind you that you are indeed the center of *your* universe and that it is perfectly self-loving to think so. As the center, you are a magnet, attracting situations, people, and things to you. Your Optimum Guide Activated or what I call YOGA is the practice of tuning into your inner guidance so that you can make decisions to maximize your well-being.

First, let's look at the word yoga in its traditional sense. Yoga literally means to "yoke" or to "link" back. What are we remembering to link back to? The answer is our divine nature. As we travel through life, we often develop a perception of being unplugged from that all-powerful source. In reality, we can never become unplugged or separated. We only lose consciousness of being one with the source. That source, which goes by many different names, is what makes the invisible visible. It is the infinite intelligence underlying the systematic operation of the universe and all of creation. When we understand the cosmos, we understand ourselves. When we know ourselves, we know the cosmos.

There is a great deal of misunderstanding and confusion about the practice of yoga. It does not belong to a particular religion. Yoga transcends religion and has been used by the ancients of many cultures to awaken their divine nature in daily living.

Anybody who is in reasonably good physical condition can practice yoga. Although there are many different styles of yoga and yogic traditions, the thread that unites the various systems is found in the intent of the practice: to reach the highest mental, physical, emotional, and spiritual potential through the remembrance of your divine connection to the infinite source, God. The goal of yoga is not to contort your body in order to flaunt or prove your physical prowess, but rather to help you remember God within by allowing more energy into your body. You can allow more of God's expression through yourself by controlling your breath.

PCS

Yoga practice helps grow awareness of your thoughts and how you communicate with yourself. Have you checked your personal communication system or PCS lately? No, I'm not talking about Sprint PCS, but your Personal (P) Communication (C) System (S). Personal Communication is the meaning you give to situations, circumstances, and whatever else happens in your life.

You see, your personal communication system is the repertoire of stories you tell yourself about what is happening in your life. One day while checking my voicemail at work, a woman left me a rude message because I did not return her phone call. She said that she had left several messages and that I was out of line for acting "uppity" since I was ignoring her. She ranted about how people like me get "too high and mighty" to help others. I was shocked by this tirade because that was the first message that I had received from her. She obviously was telling herself all types of stories about why I had not called her back. It did not occur to her that I had never received any of her messages. I couldn't return her call this time either because she didn't leave her name or number.

Does this sound familiar? Have you ever jumped to conclusions and told yourself stories only to find out that your thoughts about someone or a situation were completely off base? This happens more often than you realize. Your mind fills in the blanks when information is missing. Filling in the blanks shapes how you will respond. Imagine if the woman who contacted me had told herself that I was not calling her back because I was either no longer employed there or had technical difficulties, so I couldn't receive her messages. I bet the message she left would have had a totally different tone. We all have made erroneous assumptions. By taking time to listen to our PCS, we can question the stories we tell ourselves about what is happening in our lives.

Your Personal Communication System should work for you and not against you. Today, be conscious of the stories you tell yourself because they shape your reality. It only takes a few seconds to ask yourself a simple question. What story am I telling myself about this situation? Your response should bring your thoughts to light so that they can be thoroughly examined.

For example, yesterday you may have done one hundred things that you feel great about and one or two things that you may have botched. Instead of focusing on the one or two things, focus on the other things that you did well, and make the appropriate adjustments for next time.

By keeping your thoughts and energy focused on the aspects of life that are going well and that are positive and uplifting, you attract more of those moments into your life. Then you can address situations by focusing on solutions instead of problems.

We have a tendency to fight against anything that threatens us. We can, however choose to stand for something instead of against something else. Life is about sifting. You observe and sift through situations, people, things, and experiences, noting your preferences and what you would like to incorporate into your life. Then, by the attention you give to what you observe or mentally create, you draw to you, including people.

Like you, I'm responsible for what I draw to me. After completing graduate school, I relocated to Washington, DC to join my husband who worked at a federal agency. After researching nonprofit organizations, I discovered that I had a strong desire to work with an organization or company that helped other nonprofits.

When I read about the Foundation Center, a library/learning center for nonprofits and foundations, my heart danced. The Foundation Center offers a range of classes in grantseeking and nonprofit management. Although headquartered in New York, they have offices in Washington, DC. San Francisco, Atlanta, and Cleveland. I called the executive director in the Washington D.C. office. To my surprise, she answered the phone.

I said that I was a recent graduate from Indiana University's Center on Philanthropy and School of Public and Environmental Affairs. She gasped, stating that she helped to found the Center on Philanthropy. I was floored. She invited me to the library. The next week, I was there assisting with research and learning as much as I could about the Foundation Center and its resources. I had access to books, classes, and a knowledgeable staff. My time there was enjoyable. I knew that working at the Foundation Center would be a good fit with my skills.

At the end of my month of service to the Foundation Center, I landed a position at a D.C.-based staffing agency for the nonprofit sector. This was a phenomenal experience too because I had the opportunity to interview people daily and help place them in jobs. After a few months there, my husband and I relocated to Atlanta.

I landed a job as a manager for a large staffing company where I stayed for six months. I felt that my career was moving in the wrong direction. Ironically, a few weeks later, I applied for a training coordinator position at the Foundation Center-Atlanta. I e-mailed the director to let her know that I applied. Within ten minutes, I received a phone call from the New York headquarters and the interview process began. A few days later, I was hired. I drew this opportunity to me, by making the effort to reach out and to give. My tenure at the Foundation Center proved to be good fortune .

You can decide to be a blessing to every person you meet by giving her something. It can be a smile, a genuine compliment, or a silent prayer. When you give, you will receive from the universe in kind. That's the law. Even when you do not take action, but instead send out thoughts of peace, love, and harmony, you are doing something. While taking physical action is important, it is also important at times to sit and do nothing physically while directing your thoughts mentally. Set aside some time to do nothing. You don't have to travel across the country or to some plush resort to enjoy your time doing nothing. Simply relax in the comfort of your own home. If you live with other people, make sure that you let them know what you're up to so that they can support you in your efforts.

When you have a dream or goal that requires you to stretch yourself, you are naturally required to move out of your comfort zone. Moving out of your comfort zone can be frightening and can make you feel anxious or unsettled. These feelings are common. What you do about these feelings, however, is up to you. Many people shirk the responsibilities of change. The story they tell themselves is, "It is too hard; I can never do that" or, "That's just not me." At some point you have to take off the training wheels, step out on faith, face the challenge, and take the risk.

Creative process

Wallace Wattles, in *The Science of Getting Rich,* makes the statement, "The universe is abundant and creative, not limited and competitive." That sentence transformed my world view. Ever since I first heard it, I've been trying to constantly incorporate this new belief into my life. What does it mean for the universe to be creative, not limited? It simply means that there is enough in this world for people to have what they want. It's also important to note that not everyone wants the same things and yet the process of obtaining those desires is the same. If you "miss" an opportunity, be sure to take advantage of the next one. You will have others; it's all a part of the creative manifestation process. First there is a thought, then there is the process, and finally, the manifestation. When you look at everything as a creative process, you see that you are always creating your world.

Let's take something small for example: a messy kitchen. You first have a thought that you want the kitchen cleaned. Then you start to figure out how it's going to get clean. Perhaps you will do it. Perhaps you will enlist someone else in the household to do it, or you may even decide to hire someone. The point is that there are many ways the process of your desire could unfold. This process could take five minutes or five days depending on circumstances. Finally, the kitchen looks as clean as you had envisioned.

Obtaining a degree is a creative process. There is a thought. You want to earn your bachelor's degree. Then there is the process. Choosing a school, deciding on a major, enrolling, finding money to stay enrolled, registering, housing, purchasing school supplies and books, attending classes, studying, taking exams, passing exams, and the list goes on. The manifestation is walking across the stage with your college degree. Having the thought is generally not the issue. Most people can imagine the result fairly easily. It's the process that throws most of us off track.

Everything is a creative process. It is important to enjoy the creative process as much as possible because as Ben Sweetland says, "Success is a journey, not a destination." I rarely appreciated the process of anything unless it was fun, easy, or within my comfort zone. As soon as what I was doing grew out of my comfort zone, the process became painful and I dreaded doing it.

I was frustrated socially during my challenging junior year of high school. I wanted to change schools. Most days were a blur: I showed up, but was not really present. My guidance counselor was a godsend. Originally from Jamaica, she encouraged me to participate in the American Field Service Program. Every year the participants gave a presentation to the entire school about their summer, or semester abroad. I enjoyed these talks. But I never saw anyone who looked like me go to these exotic locations. Studying abroad was as foreign to me and my family as the locations themselves.

But in my junior year, two African-American students spoke, and I sat up straight to listen. I asked them more questions about their experiences but left it at that. Then, my best friend decided she was going to Costa Rica. That inspired me to go to Jamaica. I decided to repeat my senior year overseas before heading to college. Having such an exciting next step ahead of me was the motivator I needed to get through my senior year.

We are constantly engaged in the creative process, but often we only appreciate the result, not necessarily the process. If the process is believed to be too hard, complicated, or anything else, then it can outweigh the benefits of the result. Hardship can make it difficult to see the process through, especially when the manifestation takes longer than expected.

Here's what helped me appreciate the process involved in reaching my goals. First, I identified what I wanted. Second, I identified the result that I wanted to see. Next, I made enjoyment of the process a deliberate part of goal achievement. And I celebrated my progress along the way.

Once I learned to enjoy the creative process, I felt that I could do anything. It didn't mean that it would always be easy, but I now know that enjoying what I am doing makes it easier. The easier a task is to accomplish, the more you try, and the better you become. You want to do it more—and the cycle continues.

I also learned how important it is to be happy *now*. Why wait until my goal is achieved? I began to act as if I already had everything I wanted or needed. In reality, I do have everything that I need and I'm always grateful. The outside world enhances my inner world. What I truly want is to feel good, happy, joyous, and at peace. I know that when these good feelings are permeating, I am attracting more reasons to be positive. As the center of my universe, it is incumbent upon me to radiate the energy that I would like to attract.

Sometimes it is difficult to be happy in the moment. Here are a few things you can do to help yourself in times when you need a little extra boost. Change your physiology. Joyous people generally don't walk around sulking or with a scowl on their faces. They have an inviting energy behind their voice, and their posture and walk are definite yet at ease. A spectrum of feelings exists between depression and bliss. For the sake of this example, I will call depression 1 and bliss 20. You may not be able to go from 1 to 20 in an instant. But you can go from 1 to 4, depression to blah. Any improvement is progress.

What you want is important. Sometimes what we want is buried so deep within that we pretend to be clueless about what those wishes really are. We're fearful that we won't be able to obtain them. That uncertainty will cause negative emotions. If you determine that you will feel joyous and at peace regardless of the circumstances, you can eliminate the fear of experiencing negative emotions. Even if something in your reality causes you some pain, you know that you will recover in a timely manner.

Here is an activity that will help you in obtaining what you want on the psychic level. Recreate this chart in your journal and follow the instructions.

What I want	How I want to feel
In this column, write your desires.	In this column, write how you want to feel in the process of getting what you want.

By making "feeling good" your goal throughout the day, your attention is focused on attracting more good feelings. I don't agree with just doing what feels good, because at some point you are going to move out of your comfort zone, or run into obstacles that may make the process painful. But if you focus on feeling good regardless of the outside circumstances, you have transcended your physical circumstances and no longer have to face negative emotions. You can act with the goal of feeling good and positive. If you find that you slide back into a negative emotional pattern, instead of berating yourself, simply make an adjustment.

Once you recognize everything you do from making the bed to starting a business as a creative process, you can focus on enjoying the process of manifestation. If you think of your days as scenes, in which you are the director and the star, you can act confidently, feel the joy of the manifestation process, and expect the result you want to achieve.

Here are the steps to manifest your desires in a nutshell:

1. Declare what you want.
2. Focus on having and keeping a high vibration as you go throughout your day.
3. Expect and experience the result you want.

You must be deliberate about the scenes you create or even take part in. While there may be multiple people involved in your visualizations, you want to focus on how you experience situations. Your thoughts, feelings and actions must be aligned with what you are wanting. Being in alignment is like having a key to a buried treasure. The treasure is already there, you just have to wake up to it, just as you have to wake up and create for yourself. Many people are waiting for divine inspiration to take the next step in life. Don't wait; create! And document the clues and evidence of your progress along the way. Documenting is important because what you think and feel about is what you get. Therefore, you should take note of what you are manifesting.

If what you desire has yet to manifest, it may be helpful to focus on imagining it.

According to Jerry and Esther Hicks, imagination is using your mind to piece together images of the reality you wish to create. When using my imagination, I am free to pick and choose from life's garden and from my and others experiences to create something new. According to Hicks, the final stage of the manifestation or creation process is the allowing or disallowing of your good. You receive according to the level of your beliefs. The greater your belief, the more you will receive and the faster it will appear. Why? Because your actions are a result of your beliefs. If your thoughts, actions, and energies are aligned, you will manifest your desires. If you don't believe you will be successful or will achieve your desires, then the universe will respond accordingly. You will sabotage your own efforts in order to align your reality with your disbelief.

You know when you are allowing your good to flow to you by the way you feel and by the results that show up in your life. When you are feeling joyful and positive, you know that you are in the flow. When you are putting forth the effort and making progress, you are well on your way, no matter how small the steps may seem. It is vital that you are conscious of how you are feeling because how you feel either attracts what you want or attracts what you don't want. You don't repel, you only attract.

Synchronicity is also evidence of your allowing. For example, if you want to start your own business, suddenly you start meeting people who want to do the same and are taking deliberate steps to realize their aspirations. Perhaps you begin gravitating toward articles or magazines that feature entrepreneurs or you meet people who want to support you in your endeavors. These are all synchronistic signs that you are aligning with the vibration of entrepreneurship.

You may have noticed that when you wanted a new car, suddenly you began to spot more cars like the one you desired. After you bought your car, you may have noticed even more cars of that particular model. This is more evidence of being in vibrational alignment: you are allowing.

You are the Center of Your Universe

As the center of your universe, you want to be aware of what you are attracting in your life so that you can attract more of what you want and less of what you don't want.

Questions for exploration:
- What have you presently attracted that you want to keep in your life?
- What have you attracted that you want to eliminate from your life?
- How would you feel if you kept what you wanted in your life and eliminated from your life what did not work? What belief do you have that is stopping you from eliminating what you do not like from your life?

Affirmations:
- I love how it feels when I am conscious of the importance of feeling positive.
- I get excited when I think of having the financial resources, time, and flexibility to do more of what I want to do.
- I am in the process of attracting more of what I want into my life.

Action Steps:
1. Record your proof of prosperity and abundance.
2. Use the expression "I'm in the process of (state your goal)," instead of "I will (state your goal).
3. Create a vision board of pictures of your ideal life. Cut out pictures from magazines and print pictures from the Internet, to create a visual representation of your desires.
4. Create a void or vacuum (for example, if you want a new couch, get rid of the couch you have.)
5. Start giving more of what you'd like to have.

Application Question:
- As the center of my universe what would I like to continue attracting into my life?

Secret #5:
Become Your First Best Friend

You yourself, as much as anybody in the entire universe deserve your love and affection.
—**the Buddha**

Do you treat yourself like a best friend, or do you treat yourself like your worst enemy? Perhaps, like most women, you fall somewhere in between. We desire our friends and other people to respect us, to honor their commitments, to be trustworthy, and to laugh with us. Yet, many of us disrespect ourselves, don't honor our commitments, deceive ourselves, and take ourselves too seriously. We then wonder why we look so good yet feel insecure and emotionally unstable. When we give to ourselves what we seek from others, we learn to become our own best friend.

In the prologue of her book, *Radical Acceptance,* Dr. Tara Brach describes how during a college trip to the mountains her friend described how she was learning to be "her own best friend." Becoming your own best friend is important because it requires you to recognize your values and to gain self-mastery.

The ancient Egyptians left generations worldwide with a command to "know thyself." To know thyself, according to Egyptian philosophy, is to know the universe, and to know the universe is to know oneself. The aphorism, "as above, so below" embodies their belief in the unity and oneness of life. For the purposes of this chapter, to "know thyself" means not only to know your likes and dislikes, but to know your values.

Values are beliefs that guide behavior and provide direction about how you will manage yourself on life's journey. To live according to your values takes self-mastery. Self-mastery is an ever-evolving skill set that allows you to follow a command to yourself. The underlying assumption is that you are moving your life in a positive direction. Do you want to unleash abundant joy in your life? Then live consistently according to your values and become your own best friend.

Establishing values

Values are the foundation from which our perspectives and worldviews are developed. They are the result of the influences in our lives, particularly family, friends, media, and even strangers. Have you ever been positively affected by simply overhearing a conversation of complete strangers? Or perhaps someone said or did something to you out of the blue that negatively affected your thoughts and life. All of our experiences help to shape and reshape our values and affect the way we view ourselves and others.

Values are the lifelines that sustain us in the midst of triumphs and challenges. No matter how rich or famous you become, you should remain respectful of people around you. If you value service to others, you'll likely find ways to serve, even during periods of perceived financial lack and limitation. If you value health, you will incorporate some form of exercise into your life and monitor what you listen to, watch, read, and eat. If you value your spouse and children, you will devote your time and resources to ensure their well-being.

How do you discover your values? You can take assessment tests that are widely available on the Internet or in various popular self-help books. One of the easiest ways to discover your values, however, is to simply look at how you spend your time and money. Are your values and the way you spend your time and money in alignment?

Values can be divided into two categories: instrumental values and end-state values. Instrumental values govern our behavior when pursuing goals or achievement. They help us obtain something else that we want and are not necessarily ends in themselves. Instrumental values like courage, integrity, and kindness are examples of behaviors that build character, keep us aligned with spiritual principles, and foster harmony with those around us. People who have positive instrumental values help create and maintain a healthy social environment. People with negative instrumental values, such as selfishness and greed, help to foster dysfunction in society.

End-state values, on the other hand, are destinations such as happiness, joy, and peace. End-state values are worth having for themselves. As you may have already determined, a value can be both an end and a means to an end. A list of common values is below. This list is not exhaustive and should be used to stimulate thought about values that resonate with you.

Accuracy	Equality	Integrity
Adventure	Excellence	Justice
Authenticity	Faith	Kindness
Balance	Family	Openness
Beauty	Freedom	Perseverance
Calm	Friendship	Resourcefulness
Challenge	Fun	Respect for oneself and others
Change	Generosity	Security
Commitment	Genuineness	Service
Community	Gratitude	Skill
Competence	Happiness	Status
Continuous Improvement	Hard work	Timeliness
Cooperation	Health	Tradition
Creativity	Honesty	Trust
Discipline	Humor	Truth
Efficiency	Independence	Wisdom

Knowing your values helps you to become your own best friend. By aligning your actions with your values, you increase your confidence in your ability to change. When you violate a value that you hold dear, it can cause confusion and frustration. It may not always be easy to act consistently with your values. Like building muscles or learning any new skill, it takes practice. So don't get discouraged if you find yourself not treating yourself as well as you'd like. Once you realize what you are doing, you can make a change.

I'm learning to treat myself better. Although it takes work and commitment, when I invest time in myself, it pays dividends. Treating myself better means making sure I take time in the morning for prayer, meditation, and yoga. When I do this, everything else falls into place. Getting up in enough time to simply make it to work doesn't cut it for me, which means that I must nourish myself before leaving the house. I have to eat well and get a good night's rest in order to have the energy to give myself time in the morning to center myself.

Your values motivate you, guide your behavior, and harness your energy toward a definite purpose. After you discover your core values, you will better understand what is driving you to do what you do. Clarity about your values results in increased self-esteem.

The following poem by Mahatma Gandhi illustrates how your thoughts can indeed shape your destiny.

> "Keep your thought positive, because your thoughts become your words,
> Keep your words positive, because your words become your actions,
> Keep your actions positive, because your actions become your habits,
> Keep your habits positive, because your habits become your values,
> Keep your values positive, because your values become your destiny."

Self-mastery vs. self-esteem

It takes self-mastery to live our values, especially when it is inconvenient. Acting in accordance to our values, however, makes us authentic and increases our self-esteem. The difference between self-mastery and self-esteem is that the former is based on competencies while the latter is based on how we feel about ourselves and our competencies.

Self-mastery means having the skills to successfully manage and navigate your internal and external environments. Let's say, for example, you desire to drink more water and 100 percent fruit juices. You leave juice in the refrigerator at work in case you get thirsty. During the middle of the day, you become thirsty and want something other than water to drink. The soda is free and accessible and besides, you could use a pick-me-up. At this moment you are highly susceptible to drinking soda, which you have done on previous occasions. You head to the staff refrigerator. This time, however, you reach for the juice you brought earlier in the week instead of the soda. Your preparation allowed you to demonstrate self-mastery in this situation because you took charge of your internal and external environments. When done consistently, self-mastery positively affects your self-esteem. This is what learning to become your own best friend is all about.

Self-esteem consists of the fundamental opinions we have about ourselves beyond temporary experiences of highs and lows. To possess high self-esteem, you don't have to know it all. You have confidence in your ability to learn and mobilize resources. These resources can be discovering whom to go to for help, what books to read, what equipment to buy, or where to gather additional information.

People with healthy self-esteem don't allow setbacks in one area to impinge on other areas of their lives. For example, if you don't achieve the results you desire in a business endeavor and are forced to close shop, it doesn't mean that you have failed at being a parent, wife, or husband. People with healthy self-esteem understand the importance of confining setbacks to the particular instance where they occurred, while maintaining the ability to recognize underlying patterns in their lives in order to make necessary changes. In addition, people with healthy self-esteem think highly of themselves, yet know to pair their good feelings with appropriate skills and resources to complete a task or achieve a goal. They set themselves up for success instead of failure. Anthony Robbins the motivational guru, believes there is no such thing as failure. Failure, to Robbins, is simply an outcome or result. Instead of judging yourself for a perceived "failure," you can focus on accepting the feedback for what it is.

In Toastmasters, speakers constantly receive feedback from other members on their presentations. There is a formula that we use. First, we compliment the speaker on a specific action. Next, we suggest a specific way to make their presentation more effective. Lastly, we close with another specific and general compliment of their speech. This is called the sandwich method of feedback. As I worked with a group of young people in a Toastmasters' class and taught them this method of evaluation, they became more confident in giving their feedback as well as in accepting feedback. They learned that the person giving the feedback is not trying to "pick on" them, but help them to grow into a better speaker.

When sound technicians perform a microphone check, they may say something like, "Testing, testing, one two three... testing, one two three." If the system squeals or static erupts, technicians don't call the sound system stupid, lazy, unmotivated or uncooperative. They simply turn a few knobs, switches, and dials in order to obtain the quality of sound appropriate for the occasion. Our circumstances in life give us constant feedback. Instead of beating yourself up, focus on what you need to do to obtain the results that you want. Keep making adjustments and changes until you get the desired results.

It takes self-mastery to treat ourselves the way we desire to be treated by others. We expect people to honor their commitments to us, follow through in a timely manner, communicate respectfully and honestly, and value our skills and talents. Yet we often fail to meet those same standards when relating to ourselves. For example, when you plan to wake up at 5:00 a.m. to spend time in prayer and meditation, do you do it? Or do you hit the snooze button so many times that you wake up at 6:00 a.m. instead? Each time you don't honor your commitments to yourself, you unintentionally communicate your low self-regard to your subconscious mind.

It takes self-mastery to honor your commitment to yourself, especially when no one is watching. When you don't follow through with a commitment, instead of berating yourself, try to figure out how you can keep your commitment next time. What modifications or changes will you have to make? Once you know what you must do the next time in order to keep your commitment, do it. When you honor your commitments to yourself you are acting like our own best friend.

We expect other people to follow through and to honor their commitments to us. When others honor their commitments, it shows that they have high regard for themselves and most likely us. When it comes to following through for others, we'll eagerly do it with a sense of urgency, but when it comes to our own desires, we procrastinate and distract ourselves with various amusements. Steven R. Covey, in his acclaimed book *The Seven Habits of Highly Effective People,* reminds us to be proactive in order to free ourselves from consistently operating in crisis mode. In our jobs we are usually the epitome of efficiency and effectiveness. But when it comes to following through on tasks that will move us toward our dreams, we move more slowly than a blind turtle. It takes self-mastery to act with a sense of urgency for ourselves.

In addition, we are conditioned to be respectful and truthful when communicating with others and expect the same in return. But when it comes to ourselves, our conversation is often self-defeating and negative. We tell ourselves what we cannot do and what won't work—among other psychologically damaging criticisms. We are conditioned by the media, advertisers, and marketers to think that what we have is not good enough, fast enough, or classy enough. Our self-talk plays a major role in

Become Your First Best Friend

what we do. Although we experience hundreds of successes throughout the day, we tend to place our energy on the one or two things that did not go as we had planned. The more we dwell upon our perceived failures, the larger they grow in our minds and the more of that same energy we attract into our lives. Learning to focus on our successes is key to growing them.

Conversely, we sometimes think we are communicating with others when in reality we are expecting others to read our minds. Learning to communicate our needs by asking for what we want can be risky and may put us out of our comfort zones. When we are clear about what we want and articulate our needs, we may face rejection. The other person might decline our request. On the other hand, we may be rewarded beyond our wildest expectations. The universe has a way of working on our behalf for our highest good.

We demonstrate how we value ourselves by how we spend our time, talent, and treasures. There is always some aspect of ourselves that we wish we could get rid of or change. If only I had longer legs or a flatter stomach, or smoother skin, a smaller nose, or fuller lips. Do you spend your time thinking negatively about yourself or with others who drain your energy?

Consider the Parable of the Talents found in the Bible, Matthew 25:14-30. A master gave three of his servants talents or money. To one he gave five, to another one he gave two, and to the last one he gave one, "to each according to his own ability." Immediately after that he went on a journey. When the master returned to see what his servants had done with their talents, he discovered that the one who had five had obtained five additional talents. The one with two gained two more also, "but he who had received one went and dug in the ground, and hid his lord's money."

The master was pleased with them all except the servant who hid his talent. As a result, the master took the money from him and gave it to the servant who had ten. Sometimes we fall into the trap of thinking that we need more skill, more education, more time or more something else to prepare us to use our gifts. "For everyone who has will be given more, and he will have an abundance. Whoever does not have, what he has will be taken from him." It takes self-mastery in the form of courage to use your skills and talents to help others and to manifest your destiny.

I used to attend a Toastmasters' session every Thursday from noon to 1:00 p.m. Once, I scheduled another meeting at noon on Thursday, somehow, thinking that Toastmasters was 11:00 am-12:00 pm. Because the second meeting was important, I did not want to reschedule it. It was an opportunity to discuss hosting a workshop for women. My business partners at the time were surprised that I had missed Toastmasters in order to meet with them. I explained that I was meant to be with them at that time and not at Toastmasters. I went on to explain that I pray every morning for God to order my steps. Therefore, when so-called "mistakes" happen, I know that all is in divine order.

I always plan my days and weeks to the best of my ability, but I ask God each morning to be my guide. I also summon the help of my ancestors and angels to work on my behalf. I know that when I forget to do something or something does not go as planned, there is a divine reason. Sometimes plans just don't flow in the way that I had hoped. Yet inside, I'm assured that divine order prevails. Therefore, I can be kind to myself, like a best friend, instead of a bully. Who wants to be best friends with a bully anyway?

Mastering change

In order to master yourself, you will have to change. It takes work to make changes and adjustments because you may be set in your ways. By nature, change requires you to form new habits that support the behavior you desire. We will now explore how you can implement long-lasting change into your life through the Stages of Change Model.

The Stages of Change Model was developed by James Prochaska and Carlo DiClemente in the late 1970s and early 1980s after researching how smokers were able to stop. It is a model that focuses on the decision making of the individual. The model has five stages that individuals cycle through, sometimes repeating stages.

The first stage in the model is precontemplation. People in this stage are unaware or not interested in changing a particular behavior. Perhaps they have tried unsuccessfully in the past to change and have lost confidence in their ability to change. Individuals in this stage exhibit avoidance behavior. They do not want to think about or talk about their need to change and the consequences of their inaction. They may appear unmotivated or resistant to change.

Next is the contemplation stage in which people desire a change within a specified time frame. They are well aware of the benefits of the proposed change and the disadvantages of continuing their behavior. They perform a mental cost-benefit analysis about their change. Although the benefits outweigh the costs, people in this stage waver back and forth, procrastinating. This stage of ambivalence wastes precious mental energy that could be directed toward the intended change.

Preparation is the stage in which people have decided to embark on the road to change. This decision empowers them to plan how they intend to reach their goals and modify their behavior. Examples include joining a gym, setting up a mastermind group, or soliciting support from family and friends. Because of their willingness to change, people in this stage are open to reading self-help books and articles for inspiration and motivation. While thinking, planning, organizing, and deliberating are all part of the process of change, you must move to action in order to produce results.

During the action stage people begin to implement their plans. This leads to a demonstrable change in behavior and lifestyle. Implementing lifestyle changes is crucial to sustaining any type of change. This is also the stage where people attempt to modify their behavior without altering the way they live. Any behavioral modification should be integrated into their routines. Without this integration, individuals will fail to achieve the sustained change that they desire.

In the maintenance stage, individuals intentionally plan strategies to stay on track and to prevent relapses. Nevertheless, relapse or regression is a part of this change model. Fortunately, when people relapse, they only regress to the contemplation or preparation stage. They generally do not revert to the Precontemplation stage. Relapse is common, so don't beat up on yourself if it happens. Although the experience of relapse can be frustrating, stop yourself from spiraling down. This can lead to an emotional fallback that you can then use to rationalize return to the undesired behavior. Understanding that reverting is likely can provide comfort to those who are seriously trying to change.

Change is about stretching yourself. Stretching yourself allows you to grow beyond your boundaries. It may be very uncomfortable, but once you have stretched yourself, you will not be able to return to the same person you were before. You will have an expanded view of the world and will be able to look at situations from different angles.

Developing a winning attitude

To become your own best friend means to have a winning attitude. To persist consistently in the face of challenges propels you over obstacles. See yourself as a victor instead of a victim. It may take time before you see any changes in your situation, but if you persist, the situation must change. Remind yourself, "This too shall pass." Ralph Waldo Emerson advised, "That which we persist in doing becomes easier—not that the nature of the task has changed, but our ability to do has increased." And if we persist consistently, we are bound to become the change we wish to see in our surroundings.

In order to pass my graduate economics course I had to have a winning attitude. I had just married and moved into a newly built home. The economics course was challenging and I considered dropping the class. But it was a mandatory course, it was the last semester that I could take it, and I had to complete it. I didn't want to give up other tasks in order to devote more time and energy to my studies. After receiving my midterm grades, I knew that if I did not change, I was not going to pass the class. Eventually, I did modify my study habits; but by then, it was too late. I failed the course.

The second time around, I improved my study habits. I discovered that it took me two hours to read and understand one section of a chapter. Studying for my economics course was a part-time job in itself. But I committed to studying two hours a day, every day. Needless to say, my persistence paid off. I earned an A. It became clear to me that you have to make adjustments in your life. The less time you spend berating yourself, the more time you spend engaging in actions that will produce the results that you want.

When you embark on the journey to becoming your first best friend and prioritize your needs, some people may react negatively to the new you. Practice what I call positive selfishness. Positive selfishness means ensuring your peace, health, and well-being so that you can function better as a parent, spouse, or in any other roles you may play. Some people have no problem telling other people no. Flexing their 'no" muscle comes with effortless ease. For the rest of us, however, our "no" muscle needs strengthening.

Cathy Block and John Maniri in their book, *Power Thinking,* share an effective way to say no. Although the book is for leaders in the workplace, we are all leaders in our lives, so the advice is transferable to our daily living. First, they highlight the importance of saying yes to "tasks that stretch your abilities or actualize the ideals which you want to achieve as a leader." In order to say no effectively, you first need to identify why you want to say yes before you reflexively respond. We often say yes automatically without thinking because we have been conditioned to feel discomfort when there is silence during a conversation. Or we simply feel pressured to give an answer on the spot. To avoid saying yes to too many requests, they recommend answering requests with: "The reason I tend to want to say yes is because…." Making this statement habitual will decrease the occasions that sweep you into commitments you later wish you had not made.

Make laughter your medicine

Best friends typically share a common sense of humor. They can freely laugh *with* one another and *at* one another because trust has been established in the relationship. They know each other well enough to know when it is okay to joke around or when the other could use a hug and some encouraging words. Relationships are important to our well-being. There is nothing like having good friends with whom to share life's predictable and unpredictable moments.

When you become your own best friend, you learn to keep joy alive in your life by not taking yourself too seriously. When things are not going your way, it is easy to become discouraged. If discouragement is left unchecked, it can sour your disposition and have a negative impact on your perceptions.

Norman Cousins, although famous for his career as a journalist and editor, is probably most well-known as the man who cured himself of a debilitating disease through the use of humor. In 1976, the *New England Journal of Medicine* published his article detailing how, after learning about his rare disease, he left the hospital to heal himself at a hotel. There he took megadoses of vitamin C and watched funny movies and shows. He found that ten minutes of hearty laughter helped him sleep peacefully for two hours. The more he laughed, the better he felt. He eventually healed himself and pioneered mind-body medicine in the United States.

A University of Maryland Medical Center study suggests that regular laughter helps counteract the physical effects of distressing emotions. Here are some benefits of laughter:

- Boosts the immune system
- Reduces pain through the secretion of endorphins
- Helps you and those around you deal with stress
- Lowers blood pressure
- Improves brain functioning

While these are some obvious physical benefits of laughter and having a good sense of humor, there are also mental health and social benefits as well. One mental health benefit is that you simply feel better. It's hard to be upset when you're laughing. Humor allows us to relax some of our defenses and enables us to connect better with others. Humor is rejuvenating and increases our energy. So when you're feeling tired and "need somebody to lean on," call on a friend and have a good laugh. If you miss a day of exercise, don't fret; laugh it off instead. Engaging in hearty laughter is like "stationary jogging" and is said to burn up to 400 calories an hour.

You can also try laughter yoga or a laughter club. They do actually exist. Laughter Yoga was founded by Dr. Madan Kataria, a medical physician who pioneered the movement that began in Mumbai, India in 1995. Dr. Kataria was inspired by Norman Cousins and sought a way to use yogic exercises to induce deep laughter.

People coming together with the expressed purpose of laughing, is no joke. Laughter is serious business. Sebastien Gendry was the first American to train as a certified laughter yoga teacher with Dr. Kataria. Gendry returned to the U.S. and in 2004 founded the American School of Laughter Yoga. He played a major role in helping introduce laughter yoga in the United States. He was even featured on *Oprah*. According to the web site, http://www.laughteryoga.us/ there are over 5,000 Laughter Clubs among fifty-three countries and the number continues to grow.

When we give to ourselves what we seek from others, we learn to become our own best friend. We do this by gaining self-mastery, knowing our values, honoring our commitments to ourselves, engaging in constructive thinking, and taking steps to change. Although it seems like a tall order, increasing the laugh quotient in our lives will help keep us joyous along the journey.

Questions for exploration:
- In what ways do you treat yourself like a foe instead of like your best friend?
- How can you transform those behaviors mentioned above into that of a friend?
- When is the last time you treated yourself like your best friend? Describe the situation.

Affirmations:
- I am my own best friend.
- I treat myself with compassion and understanding.
- I value my time, talent, and treasures.

Action Steps:
- Make a list of things and activities that make you feel good about yourself and start engaging in more of those activities.
- Listen to your inner voice and ask yourself if the conversation is helpful or hurtful. If it is helpful, acknowledge yourself with a congratulatory note and paste it where you can see it often. It if is hurtful, write down on a sheet of paper what you think a wise, loving person would say to you and display that note in a prominent place as well.
- Learn your preferences and choose them accordingly.
- Visualize your day before you get started and set forth the intention to treat yourself and those you encounter with respect and assertive compassion.
- Take a sheet of paper and draw a line down the middle. On the left side, write down your successes; on the right side write any adjustments you can make for next time.

Application Question:
- In what ways did you honor yourself today?

Secret #6:
Meditate to Elevate

"It is often in meditation and silent, contemplative prayer that you feel the presence of God's goodness most strongly. In this type of prayer, you take a few meaningful words and think about them and feed upon them silently."
—**Catherine Ponder**

Twenty million people in the United States have practiced some form of meditation within the past twelve months, according to a 2007 U.S. Government survey about complementary and alternative medicine. People like me are represented in those figures. I have my own definition of meditation to share with you: practices that increase awareness of the present moment, reduce stress, promote relaxation, and enhance spiritual growth. These elements are essential to well-being. Therefore, meditation is central to creating a joy-filled life.

Some people say that meditation is listening to God, while prayer is talking to God. I agree with this statement for the most part. As mentioned earlier, meditation can also be used to visualize. Listening to your inner voice through meditation provides opportunity to become aware of your mental chatter. Yet, stopping to listen to the quiet voice within scares many people. Why? Because they sometimes erroneously believe that meditation belongs to cultures different from theirs, when in fact, meditation practices can be found in various cultures. They also may believe that people shouldn't try to experience oneness with the creator or Its creation. To try is to blaspheme, leaving meditation shrouded in mystery for those sharing these or similar perspectives.

Consequently, potential practitioners are convinced by religious dogma or well-intentioned leaders that meditation is "not of God." On the other hand, there are seekers who feel like "failures" when it comes to meditation. Feelings of calm, peace, or oneness elude them.

In my first meditation session, I was shocked by my mind's persistent activity. I could not remain focused on my breath without my mind wondering, "Did I turn off the stove? Next time I'll wear socks, so my feet won't be cold. This is a long five minutes. My mind is all over the place when I should be focused on my breath!" After the session, the instructor reassured the class that with practice, quieting our mind would become easier. My teacher was right. But when my mind is agitated, it still takes a while to experience the serenity that meditation provides.

Personal benefits of meditation

Meditation helps me to strengthen my concentration. I have a longer attention span that makes completing tasks easier. In addition, I feel less mentally scattered and more emotionally balanced when I have my quiet time before leaving the house in the morning.

In the beginning, if I didn't have my quiet time in the morning, I never practiced later in the day. I now realize that I can change the trajectory of my day by stopping whatever I am doing and breathing deeply. Having an all-or-nothing type personality made the thought of regrouping in the middle of the day less attractive than starting the day fresh. Nevertheless, I have since embraced this regrouping concept.

Although meditating in the morning was helpful, after a while, I found myself on automatic pilot by afternoon. Due to my incessant mental chatter, work environment, and having to interact with many people on a daily basis, I can easily forget my connection to the source. My unconsciousness was always revealed by some type of conditioned reaction that lingered and threatened to throw me into emotional turmoil. When I am spiritually centered through prayer and meditation, my response to situations that arise is much better.

I meditate also to listen for divine guidance. When I am uncertain about a decision or need greater insight into a situation, I become still. Insights come to me in dreams, when I journal through a process, and spontaneously while engaged in mundane activities. The time I spend in silence helps me to gain clarity and contentment about allowing the process to unfold divinely, regardless of the decisions that I make.

Meditation slows my mind down so that I can be in the present moment. I love when I absorb myself in an activity or project. I enjoy being completely engrossed to the point where I lose track of time, don't want to take a break, or even stop to get a drink of water. I call this a flow experience. When I am present and engaged, I am more productive. My mind doesn't get stuck focusing on the length of my to-do list. Instead, I concentrate on the tasks in front of me. Meditating throughout the day provides me with moments of reverie so that I can return to whatever I am doing refreshed and more alert. If I have a few extra moments to spare, I enjoy writing down my thoughts. Epiphanies and "aha" moments leap out of my mind and dance onto the sacred pages of my journal.

You probably keep a journal too and have been doing so for some time. You've been consciously walking your spiritual path, doing the best that you can. When you read something that resonates with your spirit, you document it in your journal. When you are at a lecture and you hear a juicy quote, you write it down. Your friend tells you the name of a book that you "must read." You flip open your journal and jot it down so that you will remember. Soon your journal is full of strategies, words of wisdom, plans and ideas to transform not only your life, but the lives of ten of your closest friends. So what do you do once your journal is full? You purchase another one that's just as pretty, of course. And the cycle continues.

What do you do with all those nuggets of knowledge trapped on the pages? How do you integrate what you have discovered or rediscovered into your life? In other words, what strategies do you use to remember what you have learned?

When I was about five years old, I started writing and drawing on the walls at home. My mother was baffled by my actions, mainly by the fact that I had waited so long to engage in such infantile behavior. Never mind that I had a chalk board, plenty of drawing paper, and even scrap paper from the insurance company where my mother worked. I don't know why I did it then, but to this day I get a rush from writing on walls.

Now I put paper on the walls. Colorfully drawn signs are posted throughout the guest bedroom to remind me of my goals, habits I aspire to incorporate, and next steps I will take. I post my action plans and daily water intake, among other things, on the walls of this bedroom. My vision boards are displayed on the back of the door since I keep the door closed when I am inside.

I use our guest bedroom as what writer Virginia Woolf called "a room of one's own." In this bedroom, I can wake up freely at one in the morning and start writing until I feel like stopping without disturbing my husband. I can work in the bed and keep the lamp lights on. This bedroom is my private sanctuary where I can honor the impulsive needs of my spirit to create.

I have learned to take the golden nuggets out of the pages of my journal and put them in places where I can see, update, and monitor them. My postings are not static; they are living documents that I am constantly adding to and changing. Although my bedroom resembles more of a middle school classroom, it is highly functional and inspiring to me daily. If this strategy to remember does not work for you, find one that does. It's the process of finding what works and what doesn't work that makes this journey so much fun in the first place.

Another strategy involves getting the help of friends. I have friends who encourage, inspire, and push me along my path. They are a safety net bouncing me back on track when I veer off course. They reflect my inner light when I feel as if I am stumbling in the darkness, unsure and perhaps a bit afraid.

Exploring approaches to meditation

The most important aspects of meditating are choosing a technique that works best for you and then to do it regularly. If you tire easily of routine, develop a repertoire of techniques to keep your practice fresh and effective. Here are a few common meditation practices that you can start right away.

If asking you to sit still is like asking an ant to stop moving, try walking meditation. Choose comfortable shoes, leave your iPod at home, and wear appropriate attire. You want your focus on walking, not on the discomfort of your clothing. Before you start, bring your attention into your body. Begin by being aware of the motion of your feet as they hit the ground. Notice the position of your arms and neck. Listen to the rhythm of your breath as you stride along. Once you are walking at a comfortable pace, turn your attention to the beauty around you. If you are not surrounded by beauty, focus on appreciating what you can, like your ability to walk. Mentally celebrate being alive and having another opportunity to affect positively those around you. Smile at those you pass by and send them a silent prayer. As you walk, let the thoughts of your heart flow into your consciousness like a gentle stream and know that you are in tune with nature.

Many people find using a mantra or hymn during meditation helps to tame an unruly mind. Musical vibrations connect to a higher consciousness through your heart and mind. The vibration produced by chanting words or sounds of power allows you to tap into higher frequencies that deepen relaxation. The beauty of mantra meditation is that you don't have to understand the meaning of what you are saying to experience the effect.

A mantra can be in your own language. While there are many effective mantras in other languages, you can easily make up your own that can be just as effective, if not more. By repeating phrases like divine love, divine order, I am, or peace, you can access inner calm. This is your natural state of being.

Choose a word or phrase that resonates with your spirit. If you don't already have a sacred place where you go to develop your spirit, create one now. Your space doesn't have to be an entire room. It can be a corner of a room. Utilize items that make it special to you. Incense, pictures, fresh water, a holy book or candles add to the spiritual energy of your space. Since it is your space, you can do with it what you want as long as you honor it by reserving it for spiritual purposes.

Some beginners practice guided meditation. Someone guides you in quieting your mind to enhance your connection with your inner self. You can listen to these meditations in-person or on video, CD, or on the Internet. Meditation instructors can lead you to visit magical places during these sessions. They intentionally use words, sounds, and symbols like numbers, animals, and even certain fragrances that speak to your subconscious mind. The result draws out feelings of peace, love, and joy.

Meditating ten minutes each morning can help you flow throughout the day. I enjoy Barbara Faison's *Be Still CD* where you can learn to meditate in 10 minutes a day. Regardless of the situations that cross your path, you are better equipped to respond if you have set your intentions to maintain your inner peace. I'm convinced that morning meditations, in particular, help to arrange the day in your favor. When you breathe into the awareness of your divine connection, you attract circumstances that support your feelings of peace. Then you align with situations that will generate more peace within you. For example, you make it to the post office right before it closes. You attract people who want to assist you or you find yourself in the blessed position to help someone else.

Even if situations don't appear to be in your favor, they are always for your favor and your highest good. This concept may be challenging to remember in the midst of a psychological and emotional storm. But, difficult circumstances present growth opportunities to learn a lesson and heal a wound. So when you are in a pickle, ask yourself, "What lessons and blessings can I find in this situation?" It may take a little while to get to the point where we can ask this question and truly desire an honest answer. Nevertheless, ask anyway—not as a mere mental exercise to prove how spiritual you are, but as a way to open yourself to learn and heal.

Mediation is promoted as a daily practice because it lessens the intensity of life's irritations that can easily dominate your attention. This ancient practice brings spiritual awareness into your daily life, which keeps us "in the world but not of the world."

The many benefits of meditating are well-documented. We know that it reduces symptoms of stress, improves concentration, and strengthens immunity against illnesses. You can find detailed information about the benefits of meditation in books and by conducting a search on the Internet.

One way to heal wounds incurred throughout your life is to bring meditation down to earth. Recent research reflects the benefits of breathing deeply. Dr. James Gordon, a clinical professor of psychiatry at the Georgetown University School of Medicine and director of the Center for Mind-Body Medicine in Washington, D.C. maintains that slow, deep breathing is probably the single best anti-stress medicine we have. When you bring air down into the lower portion of the lungs, where oxygen exchange is most efficient, everything changes. Heart rate slows, blood pressure decreases. Muscles relax, anxiety eases, and the mind becomes calm. Breathing in this way also gives you a sense of control over your body and your emotions.

Dr. Andrew Weil, director of the Program in Integrative Medicine and clinical professor of internal medicine at the University of Arizona in Tucson, teaches "breath work" to all his patients. He says that the simplest and most powerful technique for protecting our health is deep breathing. He has seen remarkable results in his clients from lowered blood pressure to getting people off addictive, anti-anxiety drugs.

During meditation, you can unclutter your mind by focusing on your breath. In yogic tradition, air is the primary source of life force (prana) that permeates the universe. Breathing comes so naturally that we often take it for granted. It is so effortless that it is easy to ignore the power and effect it has on the body, mind and spirit.

When we inhale, oxygen fills the body and ignites the transformation of nutrients into energy. When we exhale, we rid the body of carbon dioxide, a toxic waste. Breathing directly affects our state of mind. It can make us anxious or calm, tense or relaxed. It can make our thinking confused or clear.

How I bring meditation down to earth

Silence is the language of the soul. When you go to that quiet place within yourself during meditation, you are enabling yourself to commune with spirit and to be unified with the universal energy field. In Isaiah 30:15 the Bible tells us, "In quietness and confidence shall be your strength." This verse embodies the wisdom of practicing silence. When you are silent, you harness your energy so it is not dissipated through conversation and the judgments of others. When you are silent, you do not have to spend time explaining, defending, or rationalizing your efforts to well-meaning people. Instead, your energy is directed toward fulfilling a definite purpose.

Society keeps our minds stimulated and focused on externals. Exercise, shopping, eating, and sex are good diversions from listening to your inner voice of wisdom. You are unable to hear your inner shaman summoning your attention. It is easy to get engrossed in activities, whether real or in your head. These things that you chase are ephemeral illusions, transitive occurrences that lead to temporary feelings of happiness.

You have grown accustomed to constant noise. Beeping, humming, buzzing, talking, screeching sounds, commercial jingles, and music enter into your subconscious. You hear the noise even when you stop and are by yourself. Sometimes the stillness and quietness of being by ourselves can be unnerving, so you turn on the television just to have it on. You call a friend, to take solace in the sound of another's voice. You read to gain direction from external sources. In today's fast-paced society, the need to create time for silence has become more pronounced.

A talk fast will give you time to be quiet and listen. My sister and I know not to call my mother on Mondays unless it is a dire emergency. Monday is her day to go within and not talk. I've done several talk fasts and am consistently amazed at the thoughts and ideas that are generated because I have allowed them time to germinate in my spirit, before speaking their power away.

Twenty-four hours is ideal, but if you can remain silent for three or more hours, that is a great start. Even if you begin with ten minutes per day, remaining silent for a period of time will help you to become more conscious of your internal and external conversations. On the day you plan a talk fast you can stay at home, avoiding the temptation to speak to others for the sake of politeness. Enlist the help of your spouse, and children, so they know what you are trying to accomplish. Explain to them that you will be more than happy to speak with them at the time that you designate. If you are a single parent, ask a family member or a trusted friend to watch your children for the day. It will be well worth it. I guarantee if you incorporate talk fasts into your life, you will enhance your creative energy and improve your focus.

The hectic pace of daily living is taxing on the nervous system. Some stimulation is healthy. But too much, over an extended period of time, can affect your ability to relax, be quiet, and to go within. Your inner voice, silenced and drowned by the distractions of life, tugs at your heart, back, stomach, leg, foot, head – anything that will get your attention. It targets your weak areas to get your attention. Don't wait until you are bedridden with a disease or until your kidneys fail to listen to your inner voice. Sit down and listen to what your inner voice is communicating to you.

Practicing silence allows you to grow aware of your inner dialogue. Do you treat yourself as you would a child who needs your love, support, and encouragement? Or do you berate yourself for not being pretty enough, smart enough, talented, or enthusiastic enough? Now is the time to give yourself the nurturing that you need to move forward in your life. If you don't do it, who else will? Why should others when it is your duty to honor yourself?

Negative self-talk is counterproductive. Engaging in it is a sure way to sabotage yourself, your relationships, and your motivation. When I found myself falling into this mind-set, I bombarded myself with affirmations and focused on being grateful. While that provided temporary solace, it wasn't until I learned to identify with my inner essence that I was able to permanently alleviate my mental anguish. My inner essence is a part of the universal essence, which I refer to as God, the all powerful source. When I identify with this changeless, ever present part of my being, I realize that nothing can be added to it or taken away from it because it is already all that it is and all that it will ever be. Through practicing moments of intentional silence, you can reawaken to this eternal part of yourself.

Being silent does not mean that you are not communicating. You communicate with your breathing, gestures, and body language, as well as other nonverbal actions. Sensitive people are able to read, hear, and feel your thoughts. Because we live in a vibrational universe, thoughts are in the air. An accumulation of thoughts about self and others are recycled and stored in the aura, a field of energy surrounding objects in nature and the human body. The aura contains codes and information. When it comes into contact with another's aura, the codes and information collide or harmonize. This is one reason why you automatically like or dislike a person. You are picking up on his or her energy vibration. If the vibration is compatible with yours, you will have a tendency to like the person. If your vibrations are not compatible, you will have a reaction that causes you to have an instinctive repulsion to that person. You two will not be able to stay in each other's presence for a long period of time.

I had a friend who had strong religious beliefs. He continually tried to convince me that his religion was the right religion. Each time I left his presence, I would have a screaming headache. After I asked him not to bring up the subject of religion and he continued, I ended our relationship to preserve my health and well-being. Although he was a good person at heart, there was something happening at a deeper level that was too toxic for me to stay around. Something wasn't quite right and I had to make a change. My fight or flight defenses were activated. When I ended our friendship my headaches stopped immediately.

Power through meditation

The type of power you gain through meditation is power of your higher self over your lower self. The ancient Egyptians built the Sphinx, a colossal structure that has the head of a man and the body of a lion or animal to symbolize how intellect and wisdom should reign over the more base instincts of humankind. Base characteristics that include lust, greed, envy, jealousy, and slothfulness are lower energy vibrations. Attributes of a higher consciousness include love, patience, peace, harmony, joy, discipline and exercising the will.

Believe it or not, meditation is not a mental activity. It is an activity that you must practice to reap the benefits. Sometimes I can get so mental and heady and believe because I think, write, and talk about meditating that I'm actually doing it. The longer I go without my daily meditation, the closer to the edge of insanity I get without even realizing it. Little things begin to bother me. I get frustrated easily. My energy level goes down. I think I'm meditating when in reality I'm not.

Fortunately, meditation is about quality rather than quantity. When I fall off the meditation wagon, I get back on by creating a homemade calendar and checking off the days that

I actually meditate. Therefore I can see patterns, and be clear about how much time I spend in practice. The visuals I hang on the walls are helpful reminders.

Meditation brings you into the present. When you are fully aware, you live more consciously instead of operating on automatic pilot. Good habitual behaviors like brushing your teeth in the morning and evening, exercising regularly, and drinking water use less mental energy when they are habits. Meditating, on the other hand, increases your awareness of what you are doing, feeling, and thinking throughout the day because you remain grounded in the moment. Sometimes awareness alone is enough to change a habit. On the other hand, you have to make more strategic and calculated efforts to change.

Meditation is a communication channel to the divine. Be persistent in your efforts to meditate and by all means don't get discouraged if you find yourself distracted and your mind roaming all over the place. When you become aware that your mind has strayed, don't resist the thoughts. Simply bring your attention back by refocusing on your breath.

Turn your meditation time into a ritual. I have a favorite pair of pink footies that I like to wear during meditation so that my feet stay warm. I like to sit on my yoga mat at the foot of my bed. My simple rituals are signals to my conscious and subconscious mind that I'm about to be still. Although you can make your meditation rituals as elaborate or as simple as you wish, keep in mind that you don't want your preparation to become a barrier. You may wish to light a candle and incense to create a peaceful mood and before beginning, set your intention. You may say something like, "I am now present in this moment and am open to receiving supreme guidance."

In Psalm 4:4, the psalmist commands believers to "meditate within your heart on your bed, and be still." And in Philippians 4:8 Paul goes a step farther and tells us where to direct our attention: "Finally, brethren, whatever things are true, whatever things are noble, whatever things are just, whatever things are pure, whatever things are lovely, whatever things are of good report, if there is any virtue and if there is anything praiseworthy, think on these things."

There are various forms of meditative practices. You have probably tried several different techniques. What is most important is that you find a style that works for you. You can tell if your meditation techniques are working for you by the way you function on a daily basis. The only form of meditation that does not work for me is the meditation that I *don't* do. Meditating for 10 minutes daily has greatly affected my life. It eases my internal dialogue so I can hear my inner voice. Just as you sometimes take a break from eating by fasting, meditation is akin to fasting from talking or excessive mental activity.

Insights often come to me about people or situations. I'm able to slow down. By practicing meditation I remember my divine nature and intentionally anchor this reflection into my consciousness to experience more peace and awareness.

Life constantly conspires to assist us in learning our soul lessons. Through meditation, we awaken to the growth opportunities ever present. By bringing our awareness into the moment, we are better able to perceive the wisdom and joy inherent in life circumstances. So, we elevate our consciousness to positively touch the lives of others.

Questions for exploration:
- On a scale of 1-10, how would you rate your state of being?
- What can you do to raise the number to a 10?
- In what ways can you incorporate meditation into your life?
- What affected you most in this chapter?

Affirmations:
- I am a vessel for God's love and in every moment of life, love, wisdom, and power flows through me.
- I am one with God and am governed by divine law.
- Supreme intelligence lives within me. It cares for me and is guiding me to express the good of my soul.

Action steps:
- Set a time in the morning and in the evening to pray and read uplifting spiritual material. Read from any source that feeds your spirit.
- Start a monthly prayer circle with family and friends and host it at a different person's home each month.
- Think of people who could benefit from a prayer and put their names in a bowl. Pull out a name and pray for that person.
- Express your desires. Put forth effort to accomplish your goals, and let go with faith so that your desires will be fulfilled.
- Go on excursions to different religious institutions to expand your awareness of the beliefs and practices of others. Search for the commonalities. Don't be surprised if you leave with several golden nuggets of inspiration to help you along your journey.

Application question:
- What did you do today that demonstrated that you listened to your higher self?

Secret #7:
Co-creation Takes Place Consciously or by Default

"Positive thinking by itself does not work. Your embodied vision, partnered with vibrant thinking, harmonized with active listening, and supported with your conscious action—will clear the path for your Miracles."
—**Summer M. Davenport**

Staying conscious throughout the day is challenging because of the forces in our environment that lull us into a receptive state of mind. Advertisements on TV, radio, Internet, and blogs, along with other communication media, vie for our attention. The state of our health, the foods we consume, and the strength of our resolve all play a role in determining our mental acuity and whether or not we give media attention mongers our energy. As the well-known adage reminds us, "Where attention goes, energy flows."

Where we flow our energy is what we create in our lives. Although God gave us free will, we are on this journey to co-create our lives consciously. Co-creation describes our role in the manifestation process, in concert with spiritual laws. The good news is that if you monitor your feelings, you will have a really good sense of what you're creating in your life. You can tell by the way you feel whether or not you are adding joy to your life. It's time to wake up to the reality that we are responsible for our lives. As Jerry and Esther Hicks remind us, we either co-create consciously or by default.

When you stay connected to your feelings, you know what type of thoughts you are thinking. If you are feeling good, you are thinking thoughts that are empowering. Get into the habit of reaching for higher thoughts that make you feel good. Instead of asking God and his universe to remove obstacles, ask instead that you get stronger, wiser, and more resilient. Again focus on what you want, not on what you do not want.

How do you know when you are in alignment with what you want? Check in with your emotions; they always tell you the truth. Joy is a state of being. I know that when I am writing, I am lifted by the thoughts of writing a book that people will enjoy and find insightful. It is no longer a big homework assignment. I derive great pleasure from writing down thoughts that flow to me. I especially enjoy writing when I get into the flow. That is, when the universe appears to open up and the words flow effortlessly through me, as if I were reading from a celestial manuscript. I get joy in the creation process.

Joy through co-creation

Most people have the concept of joy backwards, saying they will be happy or joyful when a future event occurs. I noticed this tendency within myself. I always had a goal or project looming on the horizon. My mantra went something like this: When the school year begins, I'll be so happy because I will be ready for this semester. When the end of the school year gets here I'll be able to fully relax. I will be so happy when I graduate. I will be so happy when I leave for Africa. I will be so happy when I return from Africa, and then I can put down some roots and really start my life. I will be so happy when I get a "real" job so that I can take full responsibility for myself. I will be so happy when I quit this job and am able to concentrate on my book. I will be so happy... when, when, when. The end result was that

Co-creation Takes Place Consciously or by Default

I was chasing an apparition that always managed to slip though my fingers.

Finally, I got fed up of waiting. I started to be joyful, peaceful, and loving in my now. I was no longer satisfied with waiting until after "such and such" happened before I could fully embrace my good and joy. I also found that the achievement of the goal, though highly satisfying, wasn't nearly as satisfying as the anticipation of it. You hear the phrase, "success is a journey, not a destination" so many times, but I was trying to get to some illusory point that I thought would make me happy. From that moment on, I decided that I would embrace and experience the fullness of my joy in my present moments. I was no longer going to wait. Each time I made this decision, doors opened and new paths were made for me.

In *The Power of Now*, Eckhart Tolle reminds us that now is the only time we have. The next year, month, week, or the next moment, is not promised to us. A simple phone call can change the fabric of our lives. Realizing how truly precious life is, we can gain a better appreciation for each moment we live. As long as we have life, we have the opportunity to grow and to begin again.

When you are feeling joy, you activate enzymes in your body that produce healing energy. Your immune system is strengthened and your resistance level becomes higher and stronger. In order to let the good that you have been asking for into your life, you must be in a receptive state of mind, body, and spirit. An effective way to be in this receptive state is when you are feeling good. Listening to your favorite CD, volunteering, taking a relaxing bath, or getting together with friends can put you in that special, feeling place where you are in a receptive mode to co-create more easily. Esther Hicks says, "You must be in the mode of joy, or of feeling good, in order to let in the things you've been asking for. You must first get happy. You cannot work hard enough to make the things that you want happen – it is only in your attitude of joy that they do."

Strategic planning for life

Nonprofit organizations exist to solve social problems. Their missions provide them with their reason to exist while their strategic plan provides direction. Why are you here? What is your purpose? Do you have a mission for your life? If you don't know your mission, don't wait for it to fall out of the sky. Create one of your own and work with it until you receive a divine revelation.

Most business owners create a business plan before starting an enterprise. The IRS requires nonprofit organizations to submit a detailed organizational description and tentative plans for future development in order to qualify for tax-exempt status. Established nonprofits create strategic plans to move their organizations to the next level. Why not create a plan for your life? Although life may not unfold exactly as you predict, having a plan does provide direction that will help you to prioritize and make decisions along your journey.

I have a background in nonprofit management and am accustomed to conducting strategic planning with organizations. I love strategic planning because it helps to clarify the direction the nonprofit wants to go. Although the process can be laborious and time intensive, the final result is a plan that serves as a guidepost for years to come. Elements of a strategic plan include having a vision and mission, conducting an assessment, establishing goals, creating objectives, and performing action items consistent with your intentions.

Transform your vision into affirmations

In Proverbs 29:18 we learn: "Where there is no vision, the people perish." Having a vision is like using a compass to navigate through the winding roads of life. Because I want you to thrive, not merely survive, it is important that you articulate a vision for your life. By crafting a vision statement you have the freedom to co-create according to your highest ideals. What would your world look like if you could design it exactly the way that you wanted?

Co-creation Takes Place Consciously or by Default

Burt Nanus, a leading thinker in strategic planning, defines vision as a realistic, credible, attractive future for [your life] an organization. Let's explore his definition.

- **Realistic:** A vision must be grounded in reality. For example, if you are thirty, afraid of heights and suffer from vertigo, a vision of becoming an Olympic gymnast is not realistic!
- **Credible:** You must believe in your own vision. The more you believe it and act accordingly, the more others will believe too!
- **Attractive future:** You do not operate in a vacuum. You will need support from others. Does your vision inspire others to want to help you succeed in the future?

The only part of Nanus' definition that I differ with concerns the future. He believes that a vision is not where you are now. You can turn your vision into an affirmation and make it a part of your reality through your words. As I continue to grow through experiences, my vision will change and evolve. Here is my vision for my lifestyle that I turned into an affirmation.

I am so grateful & thankful now that I co-host workshops, seminars, and retreats globally to inspire and empower people to co-create their lives. I travel with my husband on some business trips and can bring our children and invite help anytime I wish, particularly when I co-host retreats. We frequently visit family and friends and host exchange students. Thank you God for this or something better and so it is!

My vision inspires me. I've also been connecting with other people who share similar aspirations, and together we're making a difference within our families and community.

Determining your mission

Someone said that if you don't know where you are going, any road will get you there. This maxim emphasizes that without a sense of purpose we are creating aimlessly. A personal mission statement briefly describes your focus. It is a guidepost for your life and a formidable second step in planning. Aim for your mission to clearly state a purpose for what you seek to accomplish by focusing on the outcomes and not the methods. For example, your purpose is not to present seminars and workshops (methods), but rather to improve the quality of life of others.

Creating a personal mission statement strengthens your clarity of purpose. You can then act on that purpose in order to bring the vision you have of your life into manifestation. If you don't know your mission, create one from your passion. It will evolve. You can always change it. My mission is to inspire and empower people to consciously co-create their lives. Although I have formulated several statements over the years, helping people to transform their lives has always been an underlying theme. When creating a mission statement, here are a few elements to keep in mind:

- Use the K.I.S.S. (keep it simple sweetie) principle. One to five sentences should suffice.
- Keep your mission positive by finding alternatives to any negative statements.
- Make sure your mission energizes and inspires you on a daily basis.

While there is no one way to write a mission statement, here is a sample template to help you get started.
"To ... [state what you want to do, be, or have] ...so that [why is this important?]. I will do this by ... [doing what?]."
Example mission statement: To demonstrate compassion and live with joy so that I can live in a state of peace while

serving others. I will do this by seeing the best in others and in all situations.

Like your vision, your mission statement is not static. It will change and evolve with you. Keep copies of your statement so that you can see your thought patterns over time.

Taking stock with assessments

You can perform your own assessment by analyzing your strengths, weaknesses, opportunities and threats. This is known as a SWOT analysis in strategic planning. Conducting a personal SWOT analysis helps you identify your assets and areas needing improvement. Once you identify your strengths, you can use and build upon these qualities to facilitate your growth and advancement. Strengths and weaknesses are internal processes that you have more direct control over, while opportunities and threats refer to environmental factors that are beyond your direct control.

Countless profile tests are on the Internet and in books that you can take to determine your character strengths, work style, leadership style, and preferences.

Being able to recognize opportunities when they present themselves is a valuable skill. Some create opportunity where there may be none apparently available. While it is important to be able to recognize opportunity, it is just as essential that you are able to perceive potential threats.

A threat is anything that can derail you from achieving your goals. Threats are potential pitfalls to avoid, like a dieter arriving at a dinner party hungry when they know they should have eaten in advance to avoid being too hungry, which often leads to making poor food choices. Instead of focusing on the threats themselves, direct your energy on how to circumvent or prevent them. Keep focused on what you desire to create instead of thinking about what you don't want to happen.

Establishing goals

Co-creating is easier when you have goals to reach. Goals provide a direction to focus your energy. They help you to make positive changes in your life if you follow through and are willing to do what it takes to achieve them. I learned goal setting as a child from my mother. In the New Year or summer, she would sit my sister and me down at our kitchen table and have us set goals for ourselves. I always enjoyed this ritual and joyously participated. Here are goals that made my list in sixth grade:

1. Come in first place in my competition (I was probably referring to an ice-skating competition in which I placed last.)
2. Go bowling more often (I was on a beginner bowling league.)
3. Gain at least five pounds to get fatter (I finally gained those five pounds and more!)
4. To stop biting my lip (I can't explain that one.)
5. To dress better (I'm still working on this.)
6. Get at least an A or B in art history
7. Get a least an A or B in computers
8. On this report card get at least a 3.0 grade

Each time I wrote my goals, my mother would ask how I planned to achieve them. "I will accomplish my goals by working harder, by paying attention in school, by going ice skating, and by eating vegetables." Although I rarely looked at the goals after first writing them, I ended up accomplishing many of them. Looking back, I wonder how much more I could have achieved had I kept my goals visible.

Keeping your goals visible and reviewing them regularly prevents you from getting too far off track and simply forgetting. Keep your goals at the forefront of your mind and not trapped on the dusty pages of your journals. Your chances of achieving them will improve.

I find that having both long-term goals and short-term goals motivate me more than having big goals that take years to fulfill. I have to balance my goal setting with shorter range goals to feel a sense of achievement and forward movement. From this perspective, short-term goals are milestones I can achieve within a year. Yet a year is still too long not to have some success. That's why I like having objectives.

Creating objectives

When you have objectives in goal setting, you establish proof of progress. You either do it or you don't. Objectives are more concrete than goals and are considered SMART: specific, measurable, attainable, realistic, and time-bound. A SMART objective for example would be to lose ten pounds in two months, while your goal could be to live an active, healthy lifestyle. The objective in the example above has all of the elements of being SMART. Let's explore each element further.

Specific- Clear objectives eliminate fuzziness. This clarity allows you to zero in on a target that moves you closer to achieving your goal.

Measurable- Quantifying your objectives make it easier to track your progress. Using the weight loss example, it's easy to determine how many pounds you have lost within two months. By attaching numbers to your objectives, whether you achieved your objective or not will be obvious.

Attainable- Though it may not be easy and most likely will stretch you, you still should expect to achieve your objective.

Realistic- While having an objective to lose ten pounds in two months is reasonable, expecting to lose the weight three days before your twentieth class reunion is not. By giving yourself the gift of time, you can accomplish more than you think! Set yourself up for success. Make your objectives realistic by setting an appropriate timeframe.

Time-bound- Objectives with deadlines attached create a sense of urgency. When you keep your deadlines to yourself, there is no accountability. If you tell a friend what your timeframe is to achieve your objective, you now have an accountability partner. This accountability keeps you moving forward.

A goal becomes more manageable when it is broken down into parts. Establishing objectives fulfills this function. But you must do more. Creating and performing action items become critical to your success.

Performing actions items

Action items are tasks that must be performed in order to achieve an objective. Executing an action plan is like eating an elephant one bite at a time. A goal, therefore, becomes less intimidating when you have objectives and a plan of action. If at some point you become unclear about your goal, write down what you are unclear about. This will help ease you back on track.

When I was in eighth grade, my English teacher had a heart-to-heart talk with me one day after class. I was involved in several extracurricular activities and the quality of my classwork had begun to suffer. The final straw came when I hastily wrote a term paper and cut pictures out of an encyclopedia to illustrate my points. My cousin had typed my paper. It was full of mistakes corrected by Wite Out.

My teacher was appalled that I would not only deface a book but would also turn in such shoddy work. I was stunned that he called me out on it! I resented that long conversation about me doing too much outside of class. I particularly resented my teacher suggesting that I cut back on some of my other activities. All I heard come out of his mouth was about what I couldn't do. I missed the part about the importance of focusing, doing quality work, and creating plans to prevent rushing at the last minute. I get it now!

Moving toward my goal

After announcing to my friends and family that I wanted to become a successful author, there was no turning back. Publishing this book was my second objective. My first was to create a blog. Publicly declaring that I was in the process of completing my first book helped me to move toward my goal because I now felt a responsibility to follow through. Although people knew that I wanted to publish a book, they did not continuously question me about it. I was able to write a few hours a week here and there. But my schedule was full, and finding time to write became increasingly difficult. I made up in my mind that I would simply have to find the time. I recruited a book coach. After observing my lack of progress, she told me to cut back on my schedule. I felt as if I were in eighth grade again. But this time it was about the quantity of work that I failed to produce rather than the quality. My book coach and other supporters prodded and cheered me on through to the finish line. I am grateful for their help. In the end, I had to develop the discipline to write consistently.

Achieving goals leads to the desire to fulfill other goals, whether they are big or small. It is not in the completion or achievement of the goal, but rather in the journey to achieve them that we allow the most life to flow through us. We either consciously or unconsciously use the law of attraction: "like attracts like." It works regardless of our knowledge or ignorance of it.

When you make a decision and act upon it, you set into motion a chain of circumstances that are in accordance with your innermost desires. As a human magnet, you are constantly drawing to you, based upon your thoughts, feelings and beliefs. If you have a disposition that radiates a certain type of energy, you will draw to you those who radiate the same energy. Just as your positive energy attracts, your negative vibrations or energy also attract. Thoughts of insecurity, fear, jealousy and hatred attract more of the same. Thoughts of peace, love and harmony attract more of the same.

It gives me peace, confidence, and joy to know that I am loved, protected, and supported by a loving God. I also have a host of angels and ancestors assisting me at every turn. This is a belief I have that works for me. I know that when things do not go my way, there is a divine reason. After I have given it my all and have sufficiently let go, that is when things open up again.

Letting go of feelings of material lack, while simultaneously expecting to obtain your desired results, is key to manifesting. Deepak Chopra refers to this process as "detachment." You stay faithful, knowing that all is in divine order without fear of missing out on your good. Decide on how you want to feel and start feeling that way. Pledge to remain in a state of joy and gratitude no matter what! Essentially, you detach from the result.

Sometimes as we journey along our life's path we face obstacles that make us forget why we chose a certain path. We may even temporarily lose sight of our purpose. We get so bogged down in the details of pursuing goals that we forget why we wanted to achieve our goals in the first place. This happens because when we are grinding to make things work, pushing and fighting our way through, we are going against the flow and are attached to the outcome. Although we may achieve the results we desire, conscious co-creation is about experiencing our good now and not waiting until some unforeseen time in the future. All that we have is now.

We flow in and out of alignment based on what is happening with us mentally. Being in positive flow allows you to attract resources and people into your life that assist you in your endeavors. When you are operating in this energy, you are better able to appreciate what is going on around you and what is happening in your own life. But if you don't like what you are co-creating in your world, you can always change what you are thinking because different thoughts yield different results.

Co-creation Takes Place Consciously or by Default

If your thinking does not change from its present level of consciousness, you will remain at the same level of being. And you will get the same results that you have always gotten and you will fee the same way that you've always felt. You must be able to take pleasure from the reality you construct and enjoy it in your mind because your inner reality will become your outer reality. This is easier said than done.

It is easy to be happy and joyful when everything is going your way. But when it is not, you can feel very frustrated and frightened. If your joy depends on what is happening on the outside you will be in for a whirlwind of a ride. Sometimes we get so caught up in focusing on what we don't have that we overlook what we do have. Your joy must come from your indwelling God consciousness. Your strategy is to see with your optimistic spiritual eyes. Trying to change outward situations is good, but going within to change your perceptions, conditionings, and attitude is the better place to begin. These results are longer lasting.

It is not what happens to you that matters, but how you respond and interpret the events in your life. When you find yourself mentally descending into dark thoughts, you can change their direction by replacing the current thought with something that feels better.

Pivoting is a useful concept that I learned from Jerry and Esther Hicks. To pivot means to turn. Therefore you can pivot away from low-vibration thoughts and focus on more positive ones. But if you find yourself pivoting too often, it means that there are underlying issues that you need to explore. Giving yourself the gift of time to explore your deep-seated feelings and beliefs is worth more than ignoring your negative thoughts. When you are focused on all your debt, for example, and not on opportunities to generate more income, you feel bad, period. When you get caught up in this vibration, ask yourself what you need to do to feel better. Then do whatever healthy thing is required to change your vibration.

Conscious co-creation is about staying focused on what you want in life. Giving praise and thanksgiving activates the law of attraction. When your mind is directed toward what you want, you have a better chance of achieving those wants versus if you are focused on what you don't want.

Cleaning is a powerful tool to move obstacles and blockages from your life. It also allows you to engage in some sort of physical activity. When I am feeling stuck, all I have to do is clean and reorganize my physical space and it usually helps me to regain my focus and sense of order. Then I state what I desire, give thanks for receiving it, and act as if that thing or state of being is mine now. What do you do to lift yourself up when you are experiencing the blues?

We have all of the power of the universe within us. We must believe, without a doubt, that it is possible to have what we desire. Stay focused on what is possible. It is one thing to say that something is possible. It is another story to believe that it is possible for you. When you know that something is possible for you, you act accordingly. You engage in behaviors that are consistent with your beliefs.

Throughout your spiritual journey, you will have the opportunity to meet many helpers, as well as detractors, along the way. Only you can decide if they are to be all helpers, all detractors, or any combination of the two. It is my belief that each person you meet along your life's journey will be a helper, whether you know this or not. The only way the person can be a detractor is if you choose to respond in a manner that is not uplifting either to your spirit or to those around you. Even when tragedy strikes, you can turn this into an opportunity or you can descend into the depths of your own mental hell. Every day that you are alive, you are granted an opportunity to begin again to attract from a new place, either consciously or by default. The choice is yours. Which will you choose?

Questions for exploration:
- In what ways can you bring greater consciousness to what you think and do?
- What benefits of right thinking would you like to reap?
- What thoughts will you have to sow to move yourself toward the results you want to achieve in your life?

Affirmations:
- I consciously co-create my life.
- I willingly take responsibility for what I have created in my world.
- Transforming my circumstances begins with me!

Action steps:

Seven represents a number of completion (seven days in a week, seven core chakras, etc.) Therefore, this final chapter closes with seven action steps instead of five. You don't have to complete each item in one sitting. Take your time and follow your heart!

- Spend at least 10 minutes meditating with soothing music of your choice. During the meditation recite the above affirmations or affirmations of your choice and visualize how you want to live your life and create a vision statement that you can refer to often.
- Organizations have mission statements and you can too! Develop a mission statement for your life. This can change over time, so don't be afraid to write from your heart.
- Make a list of your strengths and describe how you can use this information to further your mission.
- Make a list of your weaknesses and how you can minimize them.

- Write down your opportunities so you can take advantage of as well as opportunities you can create for yourself.
- Explore the threats that could possibly stop you from achieving your goals and how you will overcome them.
- Create an action plan and get moving.

Application question:
- What thoughts dominated your consciousness today?

Conclusion

I am honored that Divine spirit has used me as a vehicle of expression. Only by working with your own spirit and developing your personal connection to the Divine will you find the peace and joy that you seek. Joy cannot be found in a title, through more education, in beauty, or in brains. It dwells in the infinite well of your soul, underneath the troubled waters of doubt, shame and guilt; underneath the elation, ephemeral happiness, and pleasantness.

Now is the time, my sisters, to reclaim your queendom. Honor your spirits by living in gratitude. Order your inner world so that joy can flow outwardly, uninhibited. Choose your mood with the same deliberateness that you choose your clothes. And be prepared to do what it takes to achieve that state of mind in a healthy and productive way. Become your own best friend by honoring your commitments to yourself. Engage in activities that bring you joy and move yourself from the bottom of the list to the top. When you move yourself to the top of your priority list, pay attention to what you attract to you. If you constantly find yourself in some mess, take a look at the decisions you made that brought you to where you are today, because like attracts like.

Now that you have tools and motivation, it is time to sow consciously and reap joyously.

Pray, persist, and prosper!

www.ingramcontent.com/pod-product-compliance
Ingram Content Group UK Ltd.
Pitfield, Milton Keynes, MK11 3LW, UK
UKHW041419180426
11947UKWH00007B/213